Dead Before Their TIME

Diana Karanikas Harvey and Jackson Harvey

MetroBooks

MetroBooks

An Imprint of Friedman/Fairfax Publishers

© 1996 by Michael Friedman Publishing Group, Inc.

Library of Congress Cataloging-in-Publication Data

Harvey, Diana Karanikas.

Dead before their time / Diana Karanikas Harvey and Jackson Harvey.

      p.   cm.

Includes index.

ISBN 1-56799-284-6 (hc)

1. Motion picture actors and actresses—United States—Death.
2. Actors—United States—Death. 3. Celebrities—United States-
-Death. I. Harvey, Jackson. II. Title.

PN1998.2.H42   1996

791.43′028′0922—dc20

[B]   95-48070

CIP

Editor: Elizabeth Viscott Sullivan
Art Director: Jeff Batzli
Designer: Lynne Yeamans
Photography Editor: Emilya Naymark

Every effort has been made to record accurate facts and figures in this text, but due to the personal nature of the material covered herein, obtaining complete information regarding dates of birth and death, resting places, and other personal details was not always possible. The publisher acknowledges discrepancies among sources and welcomes correction of any factual errors.

Color separations by Ocean Graphic International Company Ltd.
Printed in China by Leefung-Asco Printers Ltd.

For bulk purchases and special sales, please contact:
Friedman/Fairfax Publishers
Attention: Sales Department
15 West 26th Street
New York, NY 10010
212/685-6610 FAX 212/685-1307

This book is dedicated to brothers:

Johnny and Billy Karanikas

and

Steve, Cy, and Thom Chambers,

all of whom died before their time

but who live on in our hearts.

Acknowledgments

The writers gratefully thank the following:

Elizabeth Viscott Sullivan, Maryanne Melloan,

the staffs at the Los Angeles and

Glendale Public Libraries,

George Leis, Alexander and Helen Karanikas,

John and Sarah Harvey,

and Rockenwagner's restaurant.

Contents

Introduction

Dead Before Their Time is a who's who of celebrities—movie stars, sports heroes, music idols, and others—who died in the prime of life, who died too young. In spite of or perhaps because of their early demise, these superstars live on in our memory and through the millions of devoted fans who still worship them despite the fact that many of them haven't walked the earth for years.

From the ill to the ill-fated, the curious to the macabre, the infamous to the unfortunate, this book chronicles the brief lives and untimely deaths of some of the most fascinating and celebrated personalities of this century.

Andy Warhol once said that everyone would enjoy fifteen minutes of fame. Gathered in the pages of this book are people whose fame lasted far longer than fifteen minutes, yet whose time ran out.

SAL MINEO, JAMES DEAN, AND NATALIE WOOD IN THE 1955 CLASSIC *REBEL WITHOUT A CAUSE*. ALL THREE PERISHED AT AN EARLY AGE.

CHAPTER ONE

Dead Men Tell No Tales

*It is a MISTAKE to
confound strangeness
with MYSTERY.
The most commonplace
CRIME is often the most
mysterious,
because it presents no
new or special features
from which DEDUCTIONS
may be drawn.*

—Sherlock Holmes in *Study in Scarlet*
by A. Conan Doyle

WILLIAM DESMOND TAYLOR'S (STANDING) MURDER REMAINS A MYSTERY.

The mysteries surrounding the celebrities featured in this chapter range from the puzzling to the astonishing. While investigations over the years have uncovered bizarre facts about their lives, to this day their deaths remain as mysterious as they were on the day they occurred.

Bob Crane

Bob Crane secured a modicum of lasting fame for his charming, wisecracking portrayal of Colonel Hogan in the sixties television hit *Hogan's Heroes*. But in 1970, after six successful seasons, the show went off the air. Crane was subsequently offered a myriad of projects, but everything he chose to do flopped and his career floundered. Only five years after *Hogan's Heroes* was canceled, he was relegated to being a guest star on the situation comedy *The Love Boat*, a ship full of has-beens. By 1978, the forty-nine-year-old Crane had moved from Los Angeles to a retirement community in Scottsdale, Arizona, where he could still make a lucrative salary in dinner theater.

On the evening of June 28, 1978, Crane performed onstage as usual,

BOB CRANE (RIGHT) AS COLONEL HOGAN WITH COSTAR WERNER KLEMPERER AS COLONEL KLINK IN THE SIXTIES' HIT TELEVISION SHOW *HOGAN'S HEROES*.

signed autographs for his fans, then met Los Angeles businessman John Carpenter, a friend who was in town that evening. The two men went out to a local bar for drinks with two female fans whom they had promised to meet after the show. Carpenter later said he left Crane alone at the Safari Coffee Shop at about 2:30 A.M. on June 29, as he had to catch a plane back to Los Angeles.

The next afternoon, Victoria Berry, an actress Crane had befriended, stopped by his apartment. There, she found Crane bludgeoned to death, the electrical cord from a video camera wound tightly around his neck. Crane's face was so distorted that Berry couldn't identify him until she saw his wristwatch.

Unfortunately, a haphazard investigation by Scottsdale police didn't reveal much about Bob Crane's murder, although it did uncover all sorts of interesting tidbits about the affable actor. Crane had a dark secret: he was a pornography connoisseur. About fifty videotapes made by Crane, involving numerous women engaged in lewd and explicit sexual acts, with and without the actor himself, were found in his apartment. According to Berry, a whole album filled with naughty photographs that she had seen earlier was missing from the death scene. And Crane's ever-present black duffle bag, a many-zippered "little black bag," also disappeared and was never accounted for.

ABOVE: THE BODY OF BOB CRANE IS REMOVED FROM HIS SCOTTSDALE APARTMENT, WHERE HE WAS BLUDGEONED BEYOND RECOGNITION. RIGHT: THE PRIME SUSPECT IN CRANE'S DEATH, JOHN CARPENTER, TALKS WITH HIS ATTORNEY IN A LOS ANGELES COURTROOM.

John Carpenter was initially the police's number one suspect and continued to be so for quite some time. In 1994, the authorities finally decided they had enough circumstantial evidence to link Carpenter to the crime. He was charged with Crane's murder and, on October 31, 1994, sixteen years after the crime, was acquitted. Today, the death of Bob Crane remains a mystery. The murderer is still at large.

Mario Lanza

When Louis B. Mayer, then-head of MGM Studios, saw Mario Lanza perform at the Hollywood Bowl in 1947, he was so dazzled that he instantly signed the golden-throated tenor to a lucrative seven-year movie contract.

Mayer virtually ignored the weight problem that had caused Jack Warner to reject the heavy tenor (who weighed more than 250 pounds [113kg]) several years earlier as a leading man as well as the singer's equally oversized ego, both of which made him difficult to work with.

MARIO LANZA MAKES HIS MOVIE DEBUT IN *THAT MIDNIGHT KISS* (1949).

Lanza made his movie debut at MGM in *That Midnight Kiss* in 1949. His next film, *The Great Caruso* (1951), was a great success and served to further inflate his self-image. When he actually quit in the middle of filming *The Student Prince* (1954) because of a poor relationship with MGM, the studio sued him. In the end, the studio used Lanza's recorded singing voice in the film and hired a thin and handsome actor (Edmund Purdom) to mouth the words onscreen. Lanza's MGM contract ended abruptly in 1957.

Finished in Hollywood and determined to maintain his wealthy lifestyle, Lanza moved his family to Italy, where he could still secure a movie deal and live like the god he evidently thought himself to be. He went on a crash diet of grapefruit spiced with diet pills and tranquilizers, which he washed down with champagne. He struck up an acquaintance with New York mobster Lucky Luciano, who was hiding in Italy from United States authorities at the time. Luciano wanted Lanza to perform for him in Naples, but Lanza never showed up for the first rehearsal. Soon after, the singer was visited by some of the mobster's henchmen, who warned Lanza not to disobey their boss. Because of his failing health or his flailing ego, Lanza sidestepped Luciano's request and checked into a clinic in Rome for another weight-loss program instead. If Lanza thought he would be safe in the hospital, he was mistaken.

On October 7, 1959, Lanza's driver came to visit him at the clinic and found him in a coma, an empty IV pumping nothing but air into the singer's veins. Although no investigation or autopsy was ever performed, Lanza's death was listed as a heart attack. Lanza was thirty-eight years old. Still no one knows how or why he actually died.

Bruce and Brandon Lee

Although he had made twenty films as a child actor in Hong Kong, kung-fu superstar Bruce Lee was "discovered" in mid-1966 at a martial arts tournament in Long Beach, California, and given the role of Kato, the manservant–martial arts expert on the 1969 television series *The Green Hornet*. The program was short-lived, but it afforded Lee notoriety. After the program's demise, producer Raymond Chow offered Lee the lead role in the Chinese low-budget action picture *The Big Boss*, which was ultimately well received in the United States. This film, along with the success of Lee's next two films, *Fist of Fury* and *The Way of the Dragon*, made him the biggest star in Hong Kong. It wasn't long before Hollywood called him back to star in a Warner Brothers action picture.

The Warner movie, *Enter the Dragon* (1973), was a huge success,

INTERNATIONAL MARTIAL ARTS SENSATION BRUCE LEE IN ACTION. MANY FANS BELIEVE HE WAS THE VICTIM OF AN ANCIENT CHINESE CURSE.

and Lee instantly became a hot property. His next film, *Game of Death*, was being shot in Hong Kong, where he lived with his wife, Linda, daughter, Shannon, and son, Brandon. But in May 1973, at the age of thirty-two, Lee collapsed on the set suffering what appeared to be a mild epileptic-clike seizure. Several weeks later, the "Fastest Fist in the East," the man whose health-oriented diet included raw beef, was dead. An autopsy proved that his brain had swollen like a balloon, yet there were no burst or blocked blood vessels. Traces of cannabis in his stomach led to reports of drug abuse.

Shortly after Lee's death, strange boxes started piling up at the police department. The boxes contained nothing but mysterious messages implicating actress Betty Ting Pei. The Hong Kong government ordered a full inquest. Ting Pei finally admitted that Lee, along with Raymond Chow, had been at her apartment before he died. She said that the actor had complained of a headache and that she had given him a tablet of a prescription painkiller, Equagesic, which contains both aspirin and meprobamate. Lee lay down to rest in her bed and Chow left; later, when she couldn't awaken Lee, Ting Pei phoned Chow, who came back to her apartment and finally called the doctor. Lee died later that night at the hospital.

Since the body had been interred by the time of Ting Pei's and Chow's accounts, eliminating the possibility of corroboration, investigators concluded that Lee had died of some sort of allergic or other violent reaction to the ingredients of Equagesic. "Death by misadventure," they called it.

Lee's fans agreed—this was definitely death by misadventure, but not by earthly misadventure. Some people theorized that Bruce had set off a deadly

LEFT: An estimated twelve thousand fans mobbed the open coffin of superstar Bruce Lee at his Hong Kong funeral on July 25, 1973. BELOW: Bruce Lee and his son, Brandon, were both destined for fame and doomed to suffer an early demise.

three-generation curse when he bought his house in Hong Kong, while others believed that Lee had revealed and exploited far too many ancient kung-fu secrets and was being punished for his imprudent actions. Some people even speculated that Lee had been poisoned by Chinese herbs or that he was the victim of the "vibrating palm," or "delayed death strike," in which a person is, simply through a touch, condemned to die at a specific time. Whatever the actor's real cause of death, the world had lost a unique, talented and vibrant young star. Bruce Lee was given a king's funeral in China and a movie star's funeral in the United States.

Lee's son, Brandon, was a troubled child, an angry loner who was obsessed with his own mortality as well as that of his father. By the nineties, however, he was a brash young man, fond of practical jokes and riding his motorcycle without a helmet, presumably having come to terms with his father's death. He was also becoming an accomplished film actor in his own right. After several costarring roles, twenty-eight-year-old Brandon accepted the part that he hoped would make him famous: the lead in *The Crow*, a story based upon a comic-book character, a rock star who comes back from the dead to avenge the murders of him and his girlfriend.

In addition to his rising career, Brandon's personal life had become happier, too. He had plans to marry Lisa "Eliza" Hutton in April 1993 after finishing *The Crow*. The wedding invitations included this now-eerie quote from Paul Bowles' novel *The Sheltering Sky*: "Because we don't know when we die, we get to think of life as an inexhaustible well...."

The filming for *The Crow* had not gone well because of a series of production snafus and minor mishaps, including one incident in which an actor, checking his gun before cameras rolled, found a live bullet in the firearm. On March 31, 1993, eight days before the scheduled end of filming, nerves were taut and tensions were high as preparations were made to shoot the scene in which Lee's character is murdered. In the scene, Brandon was to open the door holding a bag of groceries while the "bad guy," played by actor Michael Massee, was to "shoot" him by aiming indirectly at him with a .44 Magnum revolver loaded with a blank from approximately fifteen feet (4.5m) away.

Cameras rolled and action commenced. Massee pulled the trigger and fired. Brandon crumpled to the floor in a heap. When he didn't get up, crew members rushed to help him and found blood gushing from a quarter-size wound in the lower right section of the actor's abdomen. Brandon was rushed to the hospital, where, after five hours of emergency surgery, his condition quickly deteriorated and he died.

An autopsy revealed that a real .44 caliber bullet had killed Brandon Lee. Why was that bullet in the gun? Why did Massee point and fire directly at Brandon? Both questions remain unanswered. There seemed to be no motive for Massee or anyone else to kill the fledgling star, and investigations into crew negligence have yet to reveal any wrongdoing. Lee's untimely death remains inexplicable.

The Crow was pieced together using existing footage, computer imaging, and new scenes that were shot with a body double. The film was finished and released in 1994 to rave reviews. Brandon Lee was now famous.

Marilyn Monroe

After several modeling stints as a teen (including the now-famous nude photograph that appeared in the first issue of *Playboy*), twenty-year-old Norma Jean Baker was "discovered" by Ben Lyon, a talent scout at Twentieth Century Fox, and put under contract to the studio in 1946. Newly divorced, she took on a new name ("Marilyn," Lyon's idea, was after a twenties' musical star, Marilyn Miller, while Monroe was Norma Jean's mother's maiden name) and a new look.

Marilyn starred in numerous motion pictures in the 1950s, including *How to Marry a Millionaire*, *Bus Stop*, *The Seven-Year Itch*, and *Some Like It Hot*. She married and divorced two celebrated men—baseball legend Joe DiMaggio and playwright Arthur Miller—and had affairs with many others, including both Robert and John F. Kennedy. She was notoriously late and temperamental on the set, and overly fond of Dom Perignon and sleeping pills at home. She had also had several aborted pregnancies and attempted suicide on more than one occasion.

By 1962, Marilyn, thirty-six, was living in a modest Brentwood bungalow, working on a new film, *Something's Got to Give*. On the night of August 5, Marilyn was at home. At 3:00 A.M., her housekeeper, Eunice Murray, who was spending the night at the house at Marilyn's psychiatrist's

THE MYSTERY SURROUNDING THE DEATH OF BOMBSHELL MARILYN MONROE ONLY ADDED TO THE MYSTIQUE OF HER ALLURE.

HOLLYWOOD LOVES A MYSTERY

Since its earliest days, Hollywood, in its zeal to cover up possible scandal, has inadvertently created some of the greatest mysteries of the twentieth century. Here are three strange tales that have never been solved.

Thomas Ince

On November 21, 1924, the *Los Angeles Times* ran the following headline: "*MOVIE PRODUCER SHOT ON HEARST YACHT.*" The story was never followed up in any paper, even though key witnesses claimed they had seen the corpse of movie producer Thomas Ince, complete with bullet hole.

Thomas Ince, known as "The Father of the Western," was a close friend of newspaper mogul William Randolph Hearst and his mistress, Marion Davies. On November 19, Ince boarded the Hearst yacht. Little did he know he was stepping into a spat between Hearst, with whom Davies had carried on a long-term affair, and Charlie Chaplin, with whom it had been rumored she was having a fling as well. Allegedly, Hearst, in a fit of rage, tried to shoot Chaplin but hit Ince instead. The authorities drew a different conclusion from their "investigation," in which they interviewed only one witness, a very close friend of Hearst's, then declared that the young producer had died of heart failure. Despite Ince's "innocent" demise, Hearst took it upon himself to establish a trust fund and to build an ostentatious mansion for Ince's widow. The case was never reopened. The true cause of Ince's suspicious death will never be known.

William Desmond Taylor

The murder of dashing silent film director William Desmond Taylor was one of the first great Hollywood cover-ups. On February 2, 1922, the forty-four-year-old Taylor was found laid out on the floor of his apartment, dead of two shots through the heart. When the police arrived hours later, the apartment was hopping with activity. Studio executives, housekeepers, and actresses rushed about searching for incriminating evidence. A fire blazed in the hearth, turning valuable information into ashes. What was found—monogrammed lingerie, love letters, and pornographic photographs—destroyed the careers of two of Desmond's supposed flames, actresses Mabel Normand and Mary Miles Minter, yet shed no light on his death. There was also proof that William Desmond Taylor was really William Deane-Tanner, who had deserted a wife and family in New York City and whose brother was a fugitive from justice. Rumors of drug abuse and homosexuality only further

befuddled the police. Sixty years later, writer-director King Vidor would uncover, during his research for a movie on the subject, what is presumably the truth: Taylor was indeed a homosexual, but he was killed by a jilted female lover—Charlotte Shelby, the mother of Mary Miles Minter. No one knows why, but Vidor chose not to make the movie.

ABOVE: MABEL NORMAND WAS ONE OF WILLIAM DESMOND TAYLOR'S LOVERS. THE REVELATIONS SURROUNDING HIS DEATH RUINED HER CAREER. LEFT: DASHING WILLIAM DESMOND TAYLOR STRIKES A MENACING POSE.

own blood. An autopsy revealed that carbon monoxide poisoning was the cause of death. Despite all the possible murder suspects—her ex-husband was a bootlegger and a pimp, she was having an affair with a married man who was also her business partner, and she had just turned down mobster Lucky Luciano's request that her restaurant front a gambling establishment—Thelma Todd's death, at age thirty, was ruled an accident.

Thelma Todd

The death of actress Thelma Todd was even more baffling. The "Ice Cream Blonde" was a pert comedienne who appeared in numerous films of the twenties and thirties. But on December 16, 1935, she was found dead in a garage of her Pacific Palisades apartment, located on the hillside above the restaurant she owned with director Roland West. The circumstances of her death were highly suspect. She was found hunched over the steering wheel of her new Packard convertible, her face and her surroundings drenched in her

request, allegedly awoke with an "uneasy feeling" about the star. After knocking on Marilyn's bedroom door and getting no answer, Murray went outside and looked into the bedroom through the closed French doors. Thinking that Marilyn looked peculiar, Murray called the star's psychiatrist, Dr. Greenson. When Greenson arrived, he broke into the room and found Marilyn Monroe dead—and in an early stage of rigor mortis.

That afternoon, Los Angeles police sergeant Jack Clemmons arrived at the Monroe residence to find what, in his words, "looked like a convention." (For unknown reasons, the police weren't called until 4:20 P.M. When asked why the police hadn't been contacted earlier, Greenson claimed that permission from the movie studio publicity department had had to be obtained before they could summon anyone.) Clemmons called Marilyn's death "the most obvious case of murder" he had ever seen. Marilyn's naked body was laid out diagonally on her stomach on her bed, her arm desperately reaching for the phone, her finger on the dial. An empty bottle of Nembutal lay on the floor next to her bed, and eight or ten other empty or near-empty pill bottles were on the nightstand, including one containing another potent sleeping potion, chloral hydrate. There was no glass or container of liquid to wash down the nearly fifty pills she was supposed to have ingested. There was no suicide note.

A very incomplete autopsy showed neither pill casings nor other traces of barbiturates in her stomach. An examination of her body showed injection-type bruises on the hip and signs that she had been lying dead on her back before she somehow ended up on her stomach. Still, the coroner called her death a suicide from ingestion of a mixture of nearly fifty Nembutal with some chloral hydrate.

Nonetheless, her fans have since called her death murder, with suspects and motives running the gamut. Most of the theories involve Robert Kennedy, with whom she was supposedly on the outs, asserting he did away with her when she threatened to reveal her relationships with him and his brother as well as other Kennedy-related secrets. The story was fueled by Murray, who later claimed in an interview that Bobby had visited Marilyn on the afternoon before she died.

The bungled investigation only helped to foster confusion. Telephone records from Marilyn's home the night she died disappeared mysteriously, as did her diary. Some people believe the

BELOW: GEORGE REEVES AND HIS FIANCÉE, LENORE LEMMON, IN A HOLLYWOOD NIGHTCLUB, LESS THAN TWO MONTHS BEFORE HIS DEATH. OPPOSITE: REEVES AS SUPERMAN, "THE MAN OF STEEL"—BULLETS BOUNCED OFF HIM.

diary contained an account of her affairs with the Kennedys as well as everything the Kennedy brothers had ever told her about Castro and Cuba, or about the family's relationship to the Mafia.

Since public interest and speculation had grown overwhelmingly in the twenty years since Marilyn's death, the case was reopened by the Los Angeles district attorney in 1982. The three-and-a-half-month investigation concluded that Marilyn Monroe died of a drug overdose: an accident or a suicide. Whatever the truth may be, virtually all the parties involved are no longer alive, making further investigation difficult, if not impossible.

George Reeves

There were several party goers in George Reeves' Beverly Hills home on June 16, 1959, when Reeves, the hunky star of television's *Superman*, said he was tired and went off to bed. Lenore Lemmon, a New York showgirl who was to marry George in three days, later said she had jokingly claimed, "He'll probably go up to his room and shoot himself!" when he retired. Writer Robert Condon claimed to be asleep at the time. And party pals Carol Von Ronkel and William Bliss said they had arrived late, at 1 A.M., and that shots rang out upstairs moments later.

When the authorities arrived, Reeves was pronounced dead at the scene from a bullet wound from the .30 caliber Luger pistol he often used to play a "simulated" game of Russian Roulette. Police investigating Reeves' death claimed it was impossible to

LOST IN THE CLOUDS

Amelia Earhart

In 1932, Amelia Earhart became the first woman to fly solo across the Atlantic Ocean, an accomplishment that made her famous worldwide. In the following years, she determined to prove herself a great flier. She broke speed records, then went on to break her own records and flew solo routes that no one else ever had. On July 3, 1937, at the age of thirty-eight, she set out in her Lockheed plane with her navigator, Fred Noonan, on a trip around the world. They flew from California to Brazil, then to Africa, India, and New Guinea. But, on the trek from New Guinea to Howland Island, the longest over-water stretch, the pair disappeared without a trace, never to be found. Whatever happened to Amelia Earhart—whether she was captured by the Japanese, was actually an international spy, or was merely lost at sea—remains a mystery.

Glenn Miller

Glenn Miller, the famous big-band leader ("Moonlight Serenade" and "In the Mood" were two of his hits), had been a captain in the air force since 1942. After broadcasting over the radio in England, Miller and his band were set to move to France in December 1944. In order to arrive earlier than the band and make arrangements for them, Miller decided to cross the English Channel separately in a plane with a group of officers. In crossing that thirty-mile (18km)-wide stretch of water, the aircraft disappeared, along with all the passengers. Theories have abounded that the plane got lost and landed in enemy territory, that an aerial attack caused a crash, or that there was a collision with some sort of secret robot missile. No trace of the airplane was ever found. Forty-year-old Glenn Miller was lost in the clouds.

ABOVE: AVIATOR AMELIA EARHART, PICTURED HERE IN 1929, WAS THE FIRST WOMAN TO FLY SOLO ACROSS THE ATLANTIC OCEAN. LEFT: GLENN MILLER IN 1940. THE BIG-BAND LEADER DISAPPEARED IN 1944 WHILE ATTEMPTING TO CROSS THE ENGLISH CHANNEL IN A PLANE.

find a cohesive thread to the night's events because of the nonsensical, ever-changing testimonies of the drunken guests. Despite the questionable circumstances—the empty cartridge was found under the corpse, there were no powder wounds on the body, the angle of the wound was suspect, and there were two other bullet holes in the wall—Reeves' death was ruled a suicide. The police claimed that Reeves shot himself with a gun he had held in his right hand, even though that hand was disabled from a recent auto accident.

Reeves' tumultuous personal life fueled speculation that his death was not a suicide. Despite his marriage plans with Lemmon, Reeves had been romantically involved for the greater part of the last fifteen years with Toni Mannix, the wife of Eddie Mannix, president of the entertainment company Loews Inc. and a highly influential man with many shady dealings and connections. Both George and Toni had been receiving death threats by phone in the months prior to the actor's demise.

Reeves' mother must have had her suspicions regarding her son's death, as she hired criminal attorney Jerry Giesler to investigate the matter. Giesler's investigation revealed that two shots were fired the night of Reeves' death. "Suicides rarely have a chance to shoot twice," he quipped. However, Mrs. Reeves never had a chance to pursue the investigation. She died in

NATALIE WOOD WITH THE MAN SHE MARRIED TWICE, TELEVISION STAR ROBERT WAGNER. THE COUPLE'S LAST NIGHT TOGETHER WAS SPENT IN A HEATED ARGUMENT.

1964, immediately after the investigators released their report. The police refused to reopen the case.

Natalie Wood

Natalie Wood was afraid of the water. When she was fourteen, a director tried to persuade her to do a stunt that involved diving into the water—she

went into hysterics. Nearly thirty years later, she drowned.

Natalie Wood started acting at the age of four, as an extra in *Happy Land*. By the age of nine, she had costarred in the now-classic *Miracle on 34th Street*. In 1955, at the age of sixteen, Natalie costarred opposite James Dean in *Rebel Without a Cause*. She reached her professional apex in the early sixties with two Oscar nominations.

Natalie's personal life was tumultuous. She proved to be a man-

magnet—her liaisons included Warren Beatty and Elvis Presley—and in 1957, she married dashing young actor Robert Wagner. That marriage fell apart five years later. Natalie married again in 1969, to British scriptwriter-agent Richard Gregson, and divorced him in 1972. A year later, she remarried Robert Wagner. They had a daughter and Natalie returned to acting, primarily on television, on which her husband had a hit series, *Hart to Hart*.

In November 1981, Natalie was working on a motion picture, *Brainstorm*, when actor William Holden died. Apparently, Robert Wagner spent far too much time and energy comforting his *Hart to Hart* costar—Holden's lover, Stephanie Powers. Natalie retaliated by spending more time with her co-star, Christopher Walken. Tensions must have been high to begin with on Thanksgiving weekend in 1981, when Natalie invited Walken, whose wife had gone back east, to spend time with her and Wagner aboard their yacht, *The Splendour*.

On November 27, the three actors boarded the yacht and, along with Captain Dennis Davern, headed for Catalina Island, off the coast of California. By the next evening, the situation had indeed reached a boiling point. The vacationers took the dinghy, *The Valiant*, to shore for dinner, at which they consumed large amounts of alcohol. Witnesses stated that Natalie openly flirted with Walken in Wagner's presence. An argument began between the two men, and although it is unclear what the subject was, the spat was heated. The yelling continued all the way back to *The Splendour*. Davern retired while Natalie, Robert, and Christopher continued to "party."

Natalie left the group near midnight—whether to change her clothes, go to bed, or escape the quarreling men, it is not known. At 12:20 A.M., Davern, making his final rounds, discovered that the dinghy was missing. He, Wagner, and Walken found that Natalie had disappeared as well. Several minutes later, Wagner began searching for her in another boat. At 1 A.M., he called in the Coast Guard, then sat and continued to drink more with Davern while the Coast Guard searched for Natalie. Natalie was found at 7:44 A.M., floating face down, wearing knee socks, a blue nightgown, and a red down jacket. There were bruises on her cheek, her arms, and her hands. *The Valiant*, intact with four life jackets, floated two hundred yards (182.8m) away.

No one knows exactly why Natalie left the threesome, or if the two arguing men stayed together or if one of them followed her to her cabin. Davern's testimony is inconsistent with those of Wagner and Walken. Contradicting everyone else's testimony, a witness on a nearby boat said she had heard a woman cry for help and a man respond. In the end, however, Natalie's death was ruled accidental.

What happened to Natalie Wood that night will forever remain a mystery. Only one fact is clear—Natalie died in the water—in the cold, dark depths of her deepest fears.

RIGHT: WOOD AND WAGNER'S YACHT, *THE SPLENDOUR*, ANCHORED OFF CATALINA ISLAND, NEAR THE SITE WHERE WOOD DROWNED. INSET: CHRISTOPHER WALKEN AND WOOD ON THE SET OF *BRAINSTORM* IN 1981. WOOD DIED BEFORE THE MOVIE WAS FINISHED FILMING.

She was also one of those who worked on *Rebel Without a Cause* to suffer an untimely demise, a set of deaths so strange that it has become known as the "Rebel Without a Cause

Curse." James Dean (page 100), Sal Mineo (page 37), Nick Adams (drug overdose), producer David Weisbart (mysterious illness), and Natalie Wood all died before their time.

CHAPTER TWO

Dial M for Murder

TELEVISION

has

brought back MURDER

into the home—

where

it

BELONGS.

—Alfred Hitchcock

SAL MINEO PULLS THE TRIGGER IN *REBEL WITHOUT A CAUSE* (1955).

There is little quite as chilling as when a public figure is slain. Following are the shocking stories of stars whose lives were cut short at the hands of a murderer.

Celebrity homicide is strange. Public horror and sympathy are directly proportional to how well the artists are doing in their careers. If they die at their peak, time will stop as fans and the press pay them homage. If they die young, outrage erupts everywhere. But if they die on the downswing, sympathy will be doled out a bit more meagerly. If they are making a comeback, their past and potential are mourned. If their careers are over, they're lucky to make the papers.

Sam Cooke

Sam Cooke's life was that of a shooting star: brief yet brilliant. Born in 1935, he was a top gospel artist by 1955, and by 1957 he had a number one pop hit, "You Send Me," which catapulted him to stardom. After that, Cooke was rarely missing from the Top Forty charts, with such hits as "Chain Gang," "Wonderful World," and "Another Saturday Night."

On December 10, 1964, twenty-nine-year-old Cooke, who was married to his high-school sweetheart, went alone to a party. There he met twenty-two-year-old Elisa Boyer and offered her a ride home. But when Boyer got into the car, Cooke took her to a seedy motel in South Central Los Angeles instead. He registered the pair as "Mr. and Mrs. Cooke," then allegedly forced Boyer into a room and ripped her clothes off. When Cooke was in the bathroom, Boyer fled with most of her clothes, then called the police from a phone booth on the motel lot.

HANDSOME AND TALENTED SAM COOKE WAS SHOT AND THEN BEATEN TO DEATH BY A MIDDLE-AGED MOTEL MANAGER IN 1964.

In the meantime, according to court testimony, Cooke, wearing only a sport jacket and shoes, pounded on the office door of motel manager Bertha Franklin and demanded to know where his "wife" had gone. When Franklin refused to come out, Cooke broke the office door down and assaulted her, whereupon she managed to get her hands on a .22 rifle and shoot him three times. Although wounded, Cooke was somehow able to get up and charge at her, at which point Franklin picked up a stick and clubbed him to death. The murder was ruled justifiable homicide.

Marvin Gaye

In 1961, Marvin Gaye was discovered by Motown founder Berry Gordy, Jr. That same year, Gaye married Anna Gordy, Berry's sister, and over the next ten years enjoyed nearly constant success with more than twenty hits, including "How Sweet It Is to Be Loved by You" and "I Heard It Through the Grapevine."

He also teamed up with Tammi Terrell on two classic hits, "Ain't No Mountain High Enough" and "Ain't Nothing Like the Real Thing." But in 1967, Tammi collapsed into Gaye's arms during a concert, and three years later, following several unsuccessful operations, she died of a brain tumor. Gaye virtually disappeared for a year after her death.

Although he came back stronger than ever in 1971 with the release of "What's Going On," Gaye was besieged with personal troubles: tax problems, disagreements with Motown, and his wife's affair with singer Teddy Pendergrass. Gaye lost his recording studio to the Internal Revenue Service and filed for bankruptcy.

Although his popularity dwindled in the late seventies, Gaye rebounded in 1982 with the major hit "Sexual Healing." The erotic single catapulted the singer back onto the charts and won him a Grammy for Best Male R&B Vocal Performance.

ABOVE: MARVIN GAYE WAS BESEIGED WITH TROUBLES THROUGHOUT HIS CAREER. RIGHT: MARVIN GAYE, SR., IN A LOS ANGELES COURTROOM, APRIL 5, 1984. MARVIN, SR. WAS CHARGED WITH THE MURDER OF HIS SON.

But Gaye's cocaine abuse brought his comeback to a halt. By 1984, he was living with his parents in Los Angeles. He was doing so much cocaine that his paranoia required him to keep a great store of guns on hand. His state of mind deteriorated as his intake increased, and he spent most of his time alone in his room with his arsenal of guns. Gaye's drug use and consequent erratic behavior had made the climate at the Gaye household increasingly menacing.

On the morning of April 1, 1984, Gaye's father, Marvin Sr., entered his son's room in a bad mood. A fight between the two men ensued, as Marvin Jr. was outraged at what he perceived to be an intrusion. Gaye's mother, who was taking care of her son at the time, was able to separate them—but not for long. A few minutes later, Marvin Sr.—whom many claim was senile, deranged, and a drinker—appeared in the doorway of his son's room and shot him in the chest with a revolver. Marvin Jr. fell to the floor, and his father aimed and shot him again. Marvin Gaye, the honey-voiced tenor, was dead at age forty-four.

John Lennon

The untimely death of John Lennon, who is arguably the most influential rock figure ever, was perhaps the most shocking event in twentieth-century music history.

John Lennon met Paul McCartney in high school; the two formed the Beatles and the rest is rock and roll legend, for the Beatles created rock and roll as we know it today. At one point in early 1964, the Fab Four held the number one, two, three, four, and five spots on the U.S. charts and had seven

ABOVE: MARK DAVID CHAPMAN, JOHN LENNON'S KILLER, GIVING A PIGGYBACK RIDE TO AN UNIDENTIFIED CHILD IN 1975. OPPOSITE: JOHN LENNON AND YOKO ONO. WHILE IDOLIZED BY MILLIONS, LENNON WAS MURDERED BY ONE OBSESSIVE FAN.

----

other singles in the Top 100, not to mention the number one and two albums. Since the breakup of the Beatles in 1970, due to creative differ-

ences, no group has ever come close to this kind of popularity or influence.

In the mid-seventies, after several not-so-successful albums, John Lennon dropped out of public life to spend time with his wife, avant-garde artist Yoko Ono, and raise their son, Sean. Lennon lived in seclusion for nearly five years until, in 1980, he and Yoko announced their comeback. The pair signed with Geffen Records and released the album *Double Fantasy*. John and Yoko did a series of interviews, and a world tour was imminent.

KILLED BY OBSESSIVE LOVE

Dominique Dunne

Dominique Dunne was the daughter of journalist Dominick Dunne and the niece of writers Joan Didion and John Gregory Dunne. She and her brother Griffin (*After Hours*) both caught the acting bug. By 1982, Dominique had appeared on several television shows and, after a major role in the motion picture *Poltergeist*, was planning to star in a television series. Dunne was only twenty-two when, on the evening of October 30, 1982, her estranged boyfriend, John Sweeney, a cook at the posh Ma Maison restaurant, went to her West Hollywood apartment hoping for a reconciliation. When she rejected him, the twenty-six-year-old Sweeney strangled her until she fell unconscious. After she lay in a coma in a Los Angeles hospital for five days, her heart stopped. Sweeney served only four years of a sixty-two-year sentence and was released in 1986.

ABOVE, LEFT: DOMINIQUE DUNNE (LEFT) AND THE CAST OF THE FILM *POLTERGEIST*. DUNNE'S BOYFRIEND SERVED ONLY FOUR YEARS FOR HER MURDER. ABOVE, RIGHT: REBECCA SCHAEFFER WAS ON THE VERGE OF STARDOM WHEN SHE WAS GUNNED DOWN IN HER APARTMENT BY A STALKER.

Rebecca Schaeffer

On July 18, 1989, twenty-one-year-old Rebecca Schaeffer, best known as the costar with Pam Dawber (formerly Mindy of *Mork and Mindy*) of the television show *My Sister Sam*, was to meet director Francis Ford Coppola to read for a major part in *The Godfather III*. At 10:15 A.M., she was still in her bathrobe when the doorbell rang. The intercom in Schaeffer's West Hollywood apartment was broken, so she answered the door in person. The man who stood in her doorway was Robert Bardo, a fan who had come all the way from Tucson to track down his beloved starlet. (He had gotten her address from the California Department of Motor Vehicles.) According to court testimony at Bardo's insanity hearing, they stood and talked for a short time, then she shook his hand and closed the door. But he rang the bell again. She answered, and when she nicely told him that she was in a hurry, he brandished a gun and shot her in the chest.

Rebecca Schaeffer was pronounced dead on arrival at a local hospital. Bardo was sentenced to life in prison without parole. Because of the Schaeffer case, a law was passed in California making it more difficult to obtain private information from the Department of Motor Vehicles.

At 11 P.M. on December 8, 1980, John was returning with Yoko from a recording session to their apartment in the Dakota on Manhattan's Upper West Side. Earlier in the day, he had given an autograph to a fan, Mark David Chapman, who had flown to New York from Hawaii just to see Lennon. After receiving the autograph, Chapman spent the next six hours in front of the Dakota, reading J.D. Salinger's *The Catcher in the Rye* while waiting for the singer to return. When Lennon emerged from his limousine, Chapman shot him seven times, and seven minutes later, Lennon was dead. Why did he kill Lennon? When police arrested Chapman, they confiscated the novel. Written on the flyleaf were the words "This Is My Statement." To this day, only Chapman, now in prison for life, understands their significance.

In 1981, *Double Fantasy* won a Grammy for Album of the Year.

Sal Mineo

Sal Mineo rose to stardom by playing juvenile delinquents on the big screen. Ironically, his own juvenile delinquency was the catalyst for his acting career: the son of a Bronx casket maker, Mineo was a member of a teen gang until he was caught stealing gym equipment from his school; he had to choose between acting school and reform school to atone for his crime. He chose acting and his career quickly flourished. In 1955, at the age of sixteen, Mineo was cast in the role that would shape his short-lived career, the street delinquent Plato in *Rebel Without a Cause*. As a result of this role, Mineo received an Oscar nomination, scads of letters from adoring female fans, and the nickname "The Switchblade Kid."

SAL MINEO'S (ABOVE) MURDERER, LIONEL WILLIAMS, BOASTED ABOUT KILLING THE ACTOR TO TWO JAIL INMATES IN MICHIGAN, WHERE WILLIAMS WAS BEING HELD ON AN UNRELATED BAD-CHECK CHARGE.

By the mid-sixties, Mineo had appeared in numerous motion pictures, including *Exodus* (1960), for which he was nominated for an Academy Award, and *Cheyenne Autumn* (1965).

Offscreen, there were rumors of homo- or bisexuality. By the end of the decade, Mineo had grown up, and as is the case with many teen idols, his career was over. The acting offers stopped coming. His last role was an ape in *Escape from Planet of the Apes* (1971).

By late 1975, Mineo had turned to the stage and was in Los Angeles directing and acting in a play. On February 12, 1976, he arrived home late from rehearsal, parked his car in the garage of his West Hollywood apartment, and walked toward his door. He never made it: The Switchblade Kid was stabbed in the heart by an

FALLING STARS

Fatty Arbuckle

Scandal has destroyed many a movie career, but there has been no scandal as sordid as that of Roscoe "Fatty" Arbuckle. One of Mack Sennett's original Keystone Kops and the roly-poly star of numerous silent reels, Fatty was beloved by children and almost as popular as Charlie Chaplin. But in 1921, his career came to a screeching halt

when he was accused of the rape and murder of twenty-five-year-old model-actress Virginia Rappe, who died of what was diagnosed as a ruptured bladder after attending a wild soiree in Arbuckle's San Francisco hotel suite. The conflicting testimonies of drunken party goers had Virginia behind closed bedroom doors screaming for the 266-pound (120kg) Arbuckle to "stop." A champagne bottle became part of the rumors, making the story more grotesque.

After three separate trials, three separate acquittals, and the apologies of one jury, Fatty's career was ruined. He moved to New York, where for twelve years he wallowed in a drunken stupor. In 1933, he got a second chance, when Warner Brothers hired him to do some short comedies. But after attending a party celebrating his comeback, he died of a heart attack in his hotel room. He was forty-six.

Marie Prevost

When the movies converted to sound, it was a boom time for everyone—everyone, that is, except silent film stars. Some made the transition into talkies, but those who didn't suffered in obscurity or, worse, fell into drug and alcohol abuse or took their own lives. Marie Prevost had once been one of Mack Sennett's silent bathing beauties, a dazzling star, but by 1937, her career was long over. The thirty-eight-year-old former star had been living in near poverty for years when she was found, a few days after she died, with whiskey bottles and a whining dachshund at her side. The ravenous dog had chewed both her arms and legs to bloody stumps.

OPPOSITE: FATTY ARBUCKLE IN ONE OF HIS MANY COMEDIC ROLES. HE WAS ACQUITTED THREE TIMES OF THE MURDER OF ACTRESS VIRGINIA RAPPE. ABOVE: MARIE PREVOST IN A SCENE FROM *MAN BAIT* (1926). WITH THE ADVENT OF TALKIES, PREVOST'S CAREER WAS OVER.

LEFT: Carl Switzer makes a wish as Alfalfa in *The Little Rascals*. BELOW: Nine-year-old Bobby Driscoll, who had already appeared in nine films, leaves a Los Angeles courtroom ecstatic over the approval of his three hundred-dollar-a-week contract.

Carl Switzer and Bobby Driscoll

Child stars always seem to have a particularly hard time when, in the pain and trauma of adolescence, Hollywood discards them. Carl Switzer, who played lovable Alfalfa, starred in more than sixty episodes of *The Little Rascals* from 1934 to 1940, yet was all washed up at age fifteen and drowning in alcohol by thirty-two. A violent argument over a dog and fifty dollars led to his being shot to death in 1959.

Little Bobby Driscoll had quite a career between the ages of six and sixteen. He appeared in several Disney classics, including *Song of the South* (1948) and *Treasure Island* (1950), won a special juvenile performer Oscar for *The Window* (1949), and was the voice and figure of the animated *Peter Pan* (1953). Then puberty struck, and the Disney pixie turned into an acne-faced outcast and heroin addict. By 1968, he had been arrested several times for possession, even doing time in the Chino Penitentiary—all by the age of thirty-one. In March of that year, two children discovered his corpse in an abandoned building in New York City's Greenwich Village. Since no one could identify the body, Driscoll was buried in a pauper's grave.

Later that year, his mother identified the corpse through fingerprints.

Words to live by in Hollywood: if you are a child star, don't grow up; if you are silent, learn to talk; and if you run into scandal, run away from Tinseltown.

unknown assailant. By the time neighbors responded to his calls for help, it was too late. Mineo was dead before the paramedics arrived.

Two years of police investigation proved fruitless regarding Mineo's attacker and the attacker's motive, although theories ran rampant—from random killing to a bad drug deal to a homosexual love affair gone wrong. In 1979, however, enough evidence was collected to convict twenty-one-year-old Lionel Williams of ten robberies in West Hollywood and the murder of Sal Mineo. By then, Williams was already serving time for forgery in prison, where he bragged to a cellmate that he had killed the actor and that "it had been easy." Lionel Williams was sentenced to an additional fifty-one years in prison.

There was never any real motive for the murder of Sal Mineo. Just as his career was born of irony, so was his death. He was the victim of a senseless crime carried out by the same type of hardened juvenile delinquent he had portrayed for most of his brief but stellar career.

Sharon Tate

Sharon Tate's star was on the rise in 1969. A twenty-six-year-old former beauty pageant winner, Tate had just received great reviews for her work in the movie *Valley of the Dolls*. The gorgeous actress was married to director Roman Polanski, who had rented a fabulous estate on Cielo Drive in Los Angeles' elite Benedict Canyon to house what would soon be their little family. Sharon was eight months pregnant.

On the evening of August 8, Polanski was making a movie in London. Tate decided not to go to a party she had been invited to, in favor of spending a quiet night at home with her houseguests: Abigail Folger, heiress to the

BEAUTIFUL ACTRESS SHARON TATE POSING WITH HER HUSBAND, FILM DIRECTOR ROMAN POLANSKI.

Folger's Coffee fortune; Folger's boyfriend, Voyteck Frykowski; and Jay Sebring, a thirty-five-year-old hairdresser and drug provider to the stars.

Sebring, convinced that his own Benedict Canyon home was haunted, spent a lot of time at the Polanski home. He had been there on the day a crazed musician showed up at the entrance gates looking for the previous tenant, Terry Melcher, Doris Day's son,

who was well connected in the music business and used to live on the estate with his girlfriend, Candice Bergen. Sebring and Tate turned away the musician with the insane eyes. The musician's name was Charlie.

On Saturday morning, August 9, Winifred Chapman, the Polanskis' cleaning lady, arrived at the house on Cielo Drive. The sight that met her eyes must have filled her with a horror beyond description: the previous night, Charles Manson, the leader of a

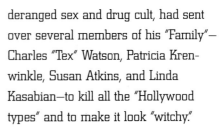

LEFT: CHARLES MANSON LEAVES THE COURTROOM AFTER BEING FOUND GUILTY OF FIRST-DEGREE MURDER OF ALL SEVEN VICTIMS IN THE TATE-LABIANCA SLAYINGS. INSET: CHARLIE'S ANGELS: SUSAN ATKINS, PATRICIA KRENWINKLE, AND LESLIE VAN HOUTEN MARCH INTO A LOS ANGELES COURTROOM IN 1970.

deranged sex and drug cult, had sent over several members of his "Family"—Charles "Tex" Watson, Patricia Krenwinkle, Susan Atkins, and Linda Kasabian—to kill all the "Hollywood types" and to make it look "witchy."

The Family had arrived at midnight. Kasabian lost her nerve and stayed outside while the others entered the house and forced the occupants into the living room. Sebring was shot. Frykowski was stabbed fifty-one times. Folger escaped out the back door, but was chased down and stabbed repeatedly. That left Sharon Tate. Watson stabbed her sixteen times, slashing her breasts and her pregnant abdomen.

To finish the act, the sadistic killers ran a rope from Tate's neck to a beam on the ceiling, then down to Sebring's neck (they covered his head with a towel first), and pulled the rope taut, like a noose. They wrote the word "PIG" on the front door in Tate's blood. The ritual was complete.

Charles Manson and all his Family members were convicted of first-degree murder. Their sentences changed to life in prison in 1972 when California abolished the death penalty.

Manson has applied for parole twice and has been denied both times. He will be eligible to apply for parole periodically for the rest of his life.

RUSS COLUMBO CROONS INTO THE MICROPHONE, THE SHADOW OF A HAND POINTING OMINOUSLY AT HIM.

Russ Columbo

In 1934, crooner Russ Columbo had two hit songs, had just signed to host his own radio show, was set to appear in two movies, and was engaged to marry the beautiful Carole Lombard.

On September 2, Columbo and Lombard had a fight, and Columbo went over to photographer Lansing V. Brown's house for consolation. The two men sat down across from each other at a desk, amusing themselves with Brown's antique gun collection while they discussed Columbo's love woes. Brown was holding a French dueling pistol with the muzzle toward the desktop when, suddenly, there was a flash. A fragment of a bullet burst out of the gun, ricocheted off the desk, went through Columbo's left eye, and lodged in his brain. A few hours later, the twenty-six-year-old singer was dead.

Elizabeth Short ("The Black Dahlia")

Elizabeth Short came to California from Massachusetts to escape a troubled home life and, of course, to become a star. Pretty and thin, her penchant for black clothing and dyed jet black hair set off a striking face, pure white skin, and haunting blue eyes. But she never

BECAUSE OF
HER DYED BLACK
HAIR AND
DARK ATTIRE,
ELIZABETH
SHORT WAS
KNOWN AMONG
HER FRIENDS
AS "THE BLACK
DAHLIA."

made it in Hollywood. By December 1946, twenty-two-year-old Short, known around the bars as "The Black Dahlia," had run out of money and turned to a life of prostitution.

On January 15, 1947, her nude body was found in the weeds along a sidewalk in Los Angeles by a woman out on a stroll with her five-year-old daughter. Upon closer inspection, it was obvious that Short had been tied spread-eagle and tortured. She had been stabbed repeatedly with a small blade and burned with a cigarette. Her mouth had been widened at the corners with a knife, her throat slit. A tattoo on her thigh had been cut out and initials carved into her other thigh. Her hair was colored red, sham- pooed, and styled. Finally, her body was severed in half, drained of blood, and scrubbed clean. Police never released all the details—they were just too gruesome. Though the case was investigated for many years by such famous law- men as "Jigsaw John" of the Los Angeles Police and Elliot Ness, Short's murderer was never apprehended.

CHAPTER THREE

Unnatural Causes

DIE?

    I should say NOT,

old fellow.

    No BARRYMORE

would allow

such a CONVENTIONAL

thing to happen

    to HIM.

    —John Barrymore

RUDOLPH VALENTINO LYING IN STATE, 1926.

Celebrities are mortal, prone to the same fatal maladies as the rest of us. This chapter outlines the tragic stories of stars who died of disease at an early age.

Florence Ballard

Florence Ballard is credited by both Diana Ross and Mary Wilson for starting the Supremes back in their days in Detroit's Brewster housing project, but when Berry Gordy, Jr., discovered the group in 1961, Ross was his main interest. Nevertheless, the Supremes became Motown's first big crossover sensation with songs like "Stop! In the Name of Love," "I Hear a Symphony," and "You Can't Hurry Love." In 1967, the hit "Reflections" was released under the name Diana Ross and the Supremes. At this point, the rivalry between Ross and Ballard, which had commenced with their Motown contract, exploded, and Ballard left the Supremes. Although Ballard is on record as having quit, many speculate that Gordy fired her. In any case, her life went downhill: she lost a lawsuit against Ross and Gordy in which she claimed she was forced out of the group, her solo career with another label floundered, and she squandered the paltry amount of royalties Motown threw her way. Just nine years after starting the Supremes with her two best friends, Florence Ballard was living on welfare in the slums of Detroit with her three children. She died of cardiac arrest on February 22, 1976, at the age of thirty-two.

FLORENCE BALLARD (LEFT) POSES WITH HER FELLOW SUPREMES, DIANA ROSS (CENTER) AND MARY WILSON (RIGHT). ALTHOUGH BALLARD STARTED THE GROUP, SHE DIED IN THE SLUMS OF DETROIT AT THIRTY-TWO.

Enrico Caruso

Born in Naples in 1873, Enrico Caruso produced the first recordings of his voice in 1902, and by the end of the next year, at the age of thirty, he was hired by Heinrich Conrad, the director of New York City's Metropolitan Opera, who first heard Caruso on the phonograph. The Metropolitan Opera would become Caruso's professional home for the rest of his life. He starred 622 times at the Metropolitan, playing thirty-six different roles there by the end of his career.

From 1903 until 1920, Caruso was the foremost tenor in the world. He toured, commanding fees of up to ten thousand dollars for a single performance, and recorded an enormous repertoire. He married American Dorothy Benjamin, with whom he had three children.

The hectic pace took its toll, and by the end of 1920, the great Caruso looked like an old man at age forty-seven. The magnificent tenor began to experience excruciating pain in his left side, and on December 11, a performance had to be stopped because he

was coughing up blood. Doctors diagnosed him with purulent pleurisy (later rediagnosed as peritonitis). In the months leading up to his death, they performed seven surgeries and drained his chest of pus, removing four inches (10cm) of his rib in the process. His career was deemed over, and Caruso told his family to throw away his music. On May 28, 1921, the Carusos set out for Sorrento, Italy.

Once there, Caruso traveled about his homeland, exerting himself to ex-

ENRICO CARUSO SETS SAIL WITH HIS WIFE, DOROTHY, AND THEIR DAUGHTER, GLORIA.

----

haustion in the summer heat despite Dorothy's admonitions. Finally, at the end of July, after a long hot venture to Pompeii, Caruso returned home with a young man who had begged him for an audition. Afterward, Caruso tried to sing himself. His glorious voice soared

out, incomparable and unhampered by his disease.

That night, he fell ill with a high fever. Dorothy called in two famous Roman surgeons who admonished Caruso to travel to Rome as soon as possible for another operation. For some reason, he waited a couple of days before leaving for Rome. By the time Caruso reached Naples, he became too weak to continue. Early in the morning hours of August 2, 1921, Enrico Caruso died.

Nat "King" Cole

Nat Cole gave his first performance in 1923 at the age of four, when he played piano in a talent show. By 1950, Nat "King" Cole was a bona fide pop star, his rich voice and smooth melodic style making him the first African-American artist to capture widespread public attention.

Over the next fifteen years, Cole was a recording powerhouse, with million-selling hits such as "Mona Lisa" and "Answer Me, My Love." In 1962, he teamed up with British jazz pianist George Shearing and turned to a more soul-oriented sound. All told, he sold more than seventy-five million records in his lifetime. He also appeared in several movies, including the 1964 Western farce *Cat Ballou*.

There's no telling what heights he might have reached had his days not been cut tragically short, for only a year later, on February 15, 1965, Cole succumbed to lung cancer at forty-five.

OPPOSITE: THE INCOMPARABLE NAT "KING" COLE. BELOW: JOHN COLTRANE KICKED HIS HEROIN HABIT, BUT NOT BEFORE IT HAD TAKEN ITS IRREPARABLE TOLL ON HIM.

Thanks to modern technology, Nat's daughter, Natalie, was able to sing a duet with her dead father on the single "Unforgettable," a remake of one of his hits, in 1991.

John Coltrane

One of the most influential jazz musicians of our time, John Coltrane was born in 1926 and raised in North Carolina, where he attended a Quaker school for African-Americans. At age twelve, he got his first instrument at school, a clarinet. A year later, he took

Bix Beiderbecke

Bix Beiderbecke was known primarily in the jazz world as a cornetist. Throughout the 1920s, he played with Chicago jazz pioneers King Oliver, Louis Armstrong, and Jimmie Noone. Beiderbecke was the star of the Wolverines. He also played with Charlie Straight's orchestra in Chicago and later with Frankie Trumbauer's orchestra in St. Louis. Bix's most famous ad-lib solo is on the Trumbauer record "Singin' the Blues" (1927). Other hits included "Jazz Me Blues" and "I'm Coming Virginia." Nevertheless, Beiderbecke wasn't afforded much recognition in his lifetime, for after being sick on and off for some time, he died of pneumonia at the age of twenty-eight in 1931. He became a legend posthumously, in part because of the Dorothy Baker novel *Young Man With a Horn* (1943), which was inspired by his life story.

Fats Waller

Thomas "Fats" Waller was the first musician to play jazz successfully on both the Hammond and pipe organs. But as a pianist, his delicacy and symmetry made him a jazz legend. Born in New York in 1904, he was a professional pianist by age fifteen. In the thirties, he recorded several satiric treatments of popular songs of the time, and this became his claim to fame. But he is best remembered for his more straightforward compositions such as "Ain't Misbehavin'" and "Honeysuckle Rose," both of which are classics. He also possessed a flair for comedy, a talent that landed him parts in several movies, including *Stormy Weather*, which was released just before his death. The thirty-nine-year-old Waller, suffering from severe bronchial pneumonia, died on December 15, 1943, on a train to New York from Los Angeles.

FATS WALLER SITS AT THE PIANO. HIS COMEDIC TALENT MADE HIM POPULAR; HIS MUSIC MADE HIM A LEGEND.

up saxophone at a high school instructor's suggestion and eventually revolutionized the instrument and music itself.

From his apprenticeship with Miles Davis' and Dizzy Gillespie's bands through his collaboration with Thelonious Monk and his second stint with Miles Davis to the formation of his own band, Coltrane displayed the kind of innovative talent that can only be described as genius. *Giant Steps* (1959) and *A Love Supreme* (1964) remain classics of modern jazz recordings.

Coltrane struggled with heroin addiction and alcohol abuse, but with the support of his Christian mother and his Muslim first wife, he pulled through and, in 1957, experienced a spiritual awakening that not only helped him quit doing drugs, but heightened his musical awareness.

However, life had several more setbacks in store for Coltrane. In 1959, he lost his front teeth because of the residual effects of his heroin addiction. In 1963, he was shaken by a divorce, and in 1964, he endured the tragic death of his good friend and collaborator Eric Dolphy. In 1965, Coltrane started experiencing a steady weight gain.

By 1967, he was living on Long Island with his second wife, Alice. The couple took a trip to Japan, where, his weight problem worse than ever, he developed a bad pain in his side. When he returned to America, he started planning a visit to Africa, a trip he had put off for years. But he would never take that journey—he died on July 17, 1967, of liver failure, just a few months before his forty-first birthday.

BOBBY DARIN AND HIS FIRST WIFE, SANDRA DEE, IN *THAT FUNNY FEELING* (1956).

Bobby Darin

When Bobby Darin was seven, he was chosen to play Santa Claus in his school's Christmas pageant. On the morning of the performance, he was taken ill with a high temperature and excruciating joint pain. He was diagnosed with rheumatic fever, which damaged his heart severely. He was told that it was unlikely he would live beyond twenty-one. He would be on heart medication for the rest of his life, and most poignantly, he would have to live with the knowledge that he could die at any time.

After years of practicing at home, Darin hit it big as an entertainer when he performed his song "Splish Splash" on *The Dick Clark Show* in May 1958. Bobby was twenty-two, and had lived a year longer than he was supposed to.

In addition to his early teenybopper hits like 1958's "Wear My Ring" and "Queen of the Hop," he went on to record several major adult hit selections, including the definitive version of "Mack the Knife" (1959), which pro-

pelled him to superstardom. Not content with his musical successes, he wanted to be a movie star—and became one. He had signed for $2 million in film contracts by the time he neared his twenty-fifth birthday. He had lead parts in *Pepe* (1960) and *Come September* (1962), and was nominated for an Academy Award for his role in *Captain Newman, M.D.* in 1964.

Unfortunately, Darin's personal life wasn't nearly as smooth. He was married to actress Sandra Dee (whom he divorced in 1966), with whom he had his only child, a son. He was also in and out of the hospital, with pneumonia and recurring heart fibrillations. And in 1967, when he made it clear that he was interested in seeking political office, his sister Nina revealed to him that she was actually his mother. The late Polly Darin, whom he thought had been his mother, was his grandmother, and his real father, whom Nina refused to name, never even knew of Bobby's existence. Nina had given birth to Bobby at seventeen, then passed him off to her mother for her to raise in

order to protect her reputation. This news was devastating for Bobby. Coupled with the assassination of his idol, Robert Fitzgerald Kennedy, the circumstances changed his whole attitude toward life. He started to liquidate his assets and to speak of death as though it were just around the corner.

Nevertheless, in 1969 he started his own short-lived record label, Directions; in the early 1970s, Darin signed with Motown and was playing in Las Vegas again. He also married legal secretary Andrea Joy Yeager in June 1972.

On December 10, 1973, Darin checked into the Cedars of Lebanon hospital in Los Angeles with severe heart fibrillations. He was diagnosed with congestive heart failure. On December 18, with only his sister Vee present, he slipped into a coma. The doctors tried operating on his heart, but it was too late; only a machine could keep the brain-dead performer alive. Early in the morning on December 20, his sister gave permission, and the plug was pulled on thirty-seven-year-old Bobby Darin.

Cass Elliot

Cass Elliot, best remembered as one of the Mamas and the Papas, a sixties folk-rock band, provided the group with a vocal talent as large as her ample girth. In their two years of existence, the Mamas and the Papas had six of their songs hit the Top Five. Their music is still played on the radio today, classic rock songs of a foregone era—"California Dreamin'," "Monday, Monday," and "Dedicated to the One I Love," among others. Their album *If You Can Believe Your Eyes and Ears* went gold. They also participated in the

CASS ELLIOT'S GIRTH CREATED BIZARRE SPECULATION AS TO THE CAUSE OF HER DEATH.

historic Monterey Pop Festival in 1967, a monumental event that their band leader, John Phillips, helped to bankroll.

By 1968, there was general disagreement among the band members, who were in a dispute with their record company, Dunhill, for breach of contract. John and Michelle Phillips were also having marital problems and subsequently divorced. The band disintegrated and all the Mamas and Papas went their separate ways.

Elliot managed to avoid the fallout from the legal dispute and continued to record on Dunhill. However, her solo career floundered and she sank into oblivion. On July 29, 1974, the thirty-one-year-old Elliot was found dead in her London apartment. A rumor quickly spread that Elliot had choked to death, either on a ham sandwich or a chicken bone. Her demise was only partially due to overeating, for Cass Elliot died of a heart attack.

Andres Escobar

One of the most popular soccer players in Latin America, Andres Escobar had much to look forward to in the 1994 World Cup. The Colombian national team was one of the favorites to go to the title game, and Escobar, a bachelor whose dark good looks made him a sex symbol in his country and earned him endorsements and spots in television commercials, also wrote a column for one of Bogotá's daily newspapers, *El Tiempo*.

The World Cup was a disaster for the Colombian team. After a 3–1 upset by the Romanian team, a message was relayed to the California hotel where the team was staying. The message targeted the team's coach, Hernan Dario Gomez, and his brother, Gabriel Gomez, a defenseman on the team: "If you play Gomez against the USA, we will set off bombs against your families in Medellín." Gomez did not play.

In the most surprising upset of the World Cup, the United States team defeated Colombia when Escobar inadvertently kicked in the deciding goal—into his own team's net. The Colombian team was eliminated and was considered a national disgrace.

Escobar arrived back in Colombia a few days later. On the evening of July 1, he went to El Indio, a nightclub on the outskirts of Medellín. At 3:30 A.M., he was accosted outside the club by three men and a woman. According to witnesses, one of the men shouted, "Thanks for the own-goal, *hijueputa* [son of a whore]." Then one of the men pulled out a handgun and began firing. Escobar was shot six times. He was taken to a hospital and pronounced dead on arrival.

Humberto Munoz, a chauffeur to Santiago Gallon Henao, a local drug figure, confessed to the murder. Whether tied to organized crime or not, the murder of Escobar brought national shame to Colombia. In Escobar's last column for *El Tiempo*, he wrote, "Please, let's not let the defeat affect our respect for the sport and the team. See you later, because life goes on." Sadly, his plea was ignored.

Jerry Garcia

The Grateful Dead was one of the last remaining symbols of the spirit of the sixties' hippie movement. As a band, the Dead's only hit single out of twenty-five albums was 1987's "Touch of Gray." But if the Grateful Dead symbolized the sixties, its leader, guitarist Jerry Garcia, symbolized all that was good and all that was disconcerting about the sixties' legacy.

Jerome John Garcia had a troubled childhood. At nine, he witnessed his father drown in a fishing accident, and lost part of a finger in a woodchopping accident soon after. His mother later ran a saloon near the San Francisco waterfront. He didn't finish high school, but enlisted in the army at seventeen; he was court-martialed twice. After he was discharged, he studied art briefly at the San Francisco Art Institute. But music was in his blood, and along with Robert Hunter, Bob Weir, and Bill Kreutzmann, he formed his first band, Mother McCree's Uptown Jug Champions, a bluegrass quartet. In 1965, the band began using electric

JERRY GARCIA ONSTAGE IN 1987.

EATING DISORDERS

Unfortunately, the chronically obese and very underweight often die young because of the strain eating disorders put upon the body.

Dan Blocker

Dan Blocker was best known for his portrayal of Hoss on the wildly successful television series *Bonanza*. The Texas native had always been a large man. He was six feet (1.8m) tall and weighed two hundred pounds (90kg) by the age of twelve. Just as he started *Bonanza*'s fifteenth season in 1972, with an expanded character and a feature film role lined up, forty-three-year-old Dan Blocker died of a blood clot in the lung.

John Candy

When comedian John Candy was a little boy, his father died of a heart ailment. A Canadian native, John grew up to achieve notoriety performing with Toronto's Second City on the television show *SCTV*. He was well loved for his work, both on television and in such films as *Planes, Trains and Automobiles* and *Uncle Buck*. He also had a terrible weight problem that plagued him from his early twenties on; Candy stood at six feet three inches (190cm) and weighed in at over three hundred pounds (136kg). He was constantly trying to diet, attending the Pritikin Longevity Center and exercising on treadmills and stationary bicycles. He wasn't able to control his eating habit—or quit smoking, for that matter. During 1994, when he was finishing the movie *Wagons East*, he died of a heart attack in his sleep at the age of forty-four.

JOHN CANDY AS UNCLE BUCK IN THE 1989 UNIVERSAL FILM OF THE SAME NAME. CANDY'S EFFORTS TO CONTROL HIS EXCESSIVE EATING AND SMOKING PROVED UNSUCCESSFUL.

Harris Glenn Milstead ("Divine")

Harris Glenn Milstead had been taunted for his obesity from the time he was a little boy growing up in a suburb of Baltimore. His outcast status may have inspired him to create the character Divine. As the buxom, heavily made-up Divine, Milstead gained notoriety through the films of high school buddy and now-famous director John Waters, especially in Waters' cult sensation *Pink Flamingos* (1972), in

Karen Carpenter

Tipping the scales on the other end of the spectrum was Karen Carpenter, the pretty lead vocalist of the Carpenters, who suffered from anorexia nervosa. A brother-sister duo, Richard and Karen Carpenter were very successful in the seventies with hits such as "Close to You" and "We've Only Just Begun," the latter becoming a popular choice for posthippie weddings. Karen, though, had always seemed a bit unstable, and as the band's popularity waned, she began to diet herself into oblivion. In February 1983, Karen Carpenter died of complications of her disease at thirty-two.

LEFT: DIVINE WAS AS FAMOUS FOR WHAT HE ATE AS WELL AS FOR HOW MUCH. **BELOW:** KAREN CARPENTER PERFORMING WITH HER BROTHER, RICHARD.

which he-she eats fresh poodle feces. Milstead also performed on stages around the world, in theaters and cabarets. He also appeared on television talk shows and guest-starred on series, and fronted a successful band, Divine Intervention. In 1988, at forty-two, 350-pound (159kg) Harris Milstead died in his sleep of a heart attack.

DISEASE AND ATHLETES

When someone we admire primarily for his physical prowess and athletic achievement perishes prematurely because his body fails him, we are filled with a supreme sadness. Certainly no one left the movie theater with dry eyes after seeing *Brian's Song*, the film based on the life of **Brian Piccolo**, the Chicago Bears football player who lost a seven-month battle with cancer in 1970 at the age of twenty-six. Nor did anyone fail to feel deeply shocked when Loyola Marymount college basketball star **Hank Gathers** died on the court from a heart attack in 1990, or when, less than three years later, another basketball player, the Celtics' **Reggie Lewis**, was struck down by the same fatal heart malady, ventricular arrhythmia, on July 27, 1993.

his close calls with death. He had been in and out of hospitals and rehabilitation centers for more than fifteen years. He was a connoisseur of psychedelic drugs (hence the sobriquet "Captain Trips"), had a bad cocaine habit, flirted

instruments and changed their name to the Warlocks. A year later, with the addition of Phil Lesh, the band became the Grateful Dead—a moniker based upon an old English fable about a reluctant corpse that Garcia picked out of the *Oxford English Dictionary*.

The Dead became the official band of writer Ken Kesey's (*One Flew Over the Cuckoo's Nest*) Merry Pranksters. The band also attracted a following like no other. Over the Grateful Dead's twenty years together, fans, known as Deadheads, followed the band around the country, traded home recordings of their concerts, and kept the sixties' spirit of communal experience alive. Joseph Campbell once said the Deadheads "were the most recently developed tribe on the planet."

Despite the band's popularity and his enormous talent, Garcia was a noted substance abuser. In fact, his drug abuse was legendary as were

with heroin on and off, and smoked three packs of cigarettes a day. In 1986 he briefly fell into a diabetic coma brought on by his years of drug abuse. But regardless of his personal circumstances, he always came back—to performing and to his fans, who, despite the band's graying, still flocked to their concerts, making the Grateful Dead the biggest moneymaking touring band in the United States. Garcia's interest in art also served him well; he designed a line of neckties that netted him millions of dollars.

In early July 1995, after another rigorous Grateful Dead tour, Garcia checked himself into the Betty Ford Center in Rancho Mirage, California, to try to beat the heroin addiction that plagued him once again. He left shortly after, only to re-admit himself into the Serenity Knolls drug treatment center in Forest Knolls, near San Francisco. During a routine bed check on August 9, 1995, a counselor at the center found Garcia in his room, dead of a heart attack. The guitarist with a truly distinctive touch was only fifty-three.

(As an interesting side note, many Grateful Dead keyboardists met early demises, too. Ron "Pigpen" McKernan died of cirrhosis of the liver in 1973; Keith Godchaux, in an automobile accident in 1980; and Brent Mydland, of an overdose of a combination of cocaine and morphine, known as a speedball, in 1990.)

Lou Gehrig

Although Lou Gehrig played most of his career in the overwhelming shadow of Babe Ruth, the "Iron Horse" was a baseball hero in his own right. His lifetime batting average was .340 with 493 home runs and 1,991 runs batted in. With the Yankees, Gehrig went to seven World Series, six of them winners for his team. His most enduring record, which stood for fifty-six years, was playing in 2,130 consecutive

"I CONSIDER MYSELF THE LUCKIEST MAN ON THE FACE OF THE EARTH." LOU GHERIG RETIRES FROM BASEBALL AT YANKEE STADIUM ON JULY 4, 1939.

games (only recently eclipsed by Cal Ripkin, Jr.). But in 1937, Gehrig's game began to deteriorate. His physical ability seemed dampened, he looked tired and old, he couldn't hit the ball anymore, and running the bases became a great strain. The 1938 season was a miserable one for him, and although he started for his team in 1939, he would break his streak and end the season prematurely, and his career forever. On May 2, in Detroit, Gehrig limped away from the playing field in obvious pain. The Iron Horse benched himself later that day.

A month later, Gehrig was diagnosed with amyotrophic lateral sclerosis (ALS), an aggressive, terminal disease that affects the brain's motor neurons, causing muscle atrophy, paralysis, and death, although the victim remains cognizant throughout the course of the disease. Lou, who had just turned thirty-six, had less than two years to live.

When Gehrig stepped up to the microphone, choked with tears, in Yankee Stadium for Lou Gehrig Appreciation Day on July 4, 1939, he must have had a sense of what was in store for him: "Fans...you may have been reading about a bad break I got. Yet today, I consider myself the luckiest man on the face of the earth....For seventeen years, I have received nothing but kindness and encouragement from you fans....I have an awful lot to live for." Gehrig did have a great deal to live for, but his days were numbered. Later that summer, the Yankees won their fourth pennant in a row—without Lou Gehrig.

During the last year and a half of his life, Lou became a complete invalid as the paralysis swept through his body, robbing him of all his strength. He could barely speak. On June 2, 1941,

No More Saturday Nights

Andy Kaufman

Andy Kaufman was the ultimate con man. The comedian's humor was a challenge: people often didn't know if he was serious or not. His stage performances featured crazy characters that didn't speak a word of English. But it was his portrayal of the goofy mechanic from Latvia, Latka Gravas, on the hit television show *Taxi* that brought him fame.

After *Taxi* went off the air in 1973, Kaufman appeared several times on *Saturday Night Live* in small set pieces. Soon after Elvis Presley died, it was Kaufman who did the first "Elvis impersonator" shtick on television. But it was the comedian's wrestling career that garnered him most of the headlines. Kaufman went on the wrestling circuit, daring and— most of the time— trouncing women who challenged him. This led to a much-publicized match with a real male wrestler, who allegedly caused him a serious neck injury.

Sadly, the gifted comedian's life was cut short by lung cancer in 1984. He was thirty-five years old.

Gilda Radner

In the mid-seventies, every Saturday night, Gilda Radner was America's favorite date. The wacky comedienne was at her peak on *Saturday Night Live*, where her goofy characters like Roseanne Roseannadanna, Emily Litella, Lisa Loopner, and Baba Wawa endeared her to a genera-

OPPOSITE: ANDY KAUFMAN AS LATKA GRAVAS ON THE SUCCESSFUL SEVENTIES SITCOM *TAXI*. ABOVE: GILDA RADNER LIT UP LATE-NIGHT TELEVISION AS ONE OF THE NOT READY FOR PRIME TIME PLAYERS ON *SATURDAY NIGHT LIVE*. SHE ONCE JOKED THAT BECAUSE OF HER FIVE-YEAR STINT ON THE SHOW, SHE DIDN'T HAVE TO WORRY ABOUT WHETHER SHE'D GET A DATE OR NOT ON SATURDAY NIGHT.

tion. But it was her valiant struggle with ovarian cancer that made her America's tragic sweetheart.

In 1973, the twenty-seven-year-old Detroit native was living in Toronto acting in local theaters when she became part of the Second City comedy troupe, joining Dan Aykroyd, John Belushi, and John Candy. In 1975, Radner, Belushi, and Aykroyd starred in the first *Saturday Night Live*, which featured such offbeat humor that the troupe was dubbed "The Not Ready for Prime Time Players."

By 1979, exhausted by the grueling schedule of putting together a weekly live show, Radner went back to the theater, this time on Broadway, starring in her own one-woman show. In 1982, while on the set of her film *Hanky Panky*, she fell in love with her costar, actor-comedian Gene Wilder. The two were married in September 1984 in the south of France. Four years later, Radner was diagnosed with ovarian cancer.

Her battle against the disease and her will to survive was inspiring. In 1988, she began writing a book about her struggle and also appeared in an episode of Garry Shandling's television show, for which she won an Emmy nomination. It was her last television appearance. On May 20, 1989, Radner died at forty-three. In mid-July of that year, her book, *It's Always Something*, reached number one on the best-seller lists.

just seventeen days before his thirty-eighth birthday, Lou Gehrig died in his sleep.

Gary Cooper won an Academy Award nomination for Best Actor for his portrayal of Gehrig in the movie *The Pride of the Yankees* (1942). Babe Ruth appeared as himself in the movie. Lou Gehrig's name didn't appear on the gargantuan posters, but Babe Ruth's did—leaving Gehrig once again in the Babe's shadow.

Amyotrophic Lateral Sclerosis is now called Lou Gehrig's disease.

Bob Marley and Peter Tosh

Bob Marley and Peter Tosh were already accomplished musicians when they met as teenagers in the slums of Trenchtown, outside Kingston, Jamaica. With Bunny Livingston, they formed the Wailers, combining reggae sound with themes of social rebellion, faith, and perseverance. The three became stars in Jamaica and emissaries of reggae and Rastafarianism the world over. In 1973, the Wailers broke up, and Livingston and Tosh went on to solo careers.

Bob Marley went on to form a new band, Bob Marley and the Wailers. The group toured Europe, Africa, and the Americas, hitting it big in England and North America with their albums *Rastaman Vibration* and *Exodus*. In Jamaica, Bob Marley was a national hero. His words, political and religious, were revered by the masses. But those with conflicting political views hated him. In 1976, he was wounded in an assassination attempt.

In late 1980, Marley set out for a tour of the United States. During one of the first concerts, he collapsed onstage.

BOB MARLEY ONSTAGE. HIS TALENT POPULARIZED REGGAE MUSIC AND JAMAICAN CULTURE.

The tour was canceled, and Marley was diagnosed with brain and lung cancer. Seven months later, on May 11, 1981, about a month after his thirty-sixth birthday, Bob Marley died.

while spending thirty minutes arguing for its legalization. Later that year, police arrested him at his studio, took him to the station, and nearly beat him to death.

Peter Tosh reached the height of his popularity in 1978, when he signed on to the Rolling Stones' record label, Rolling Stones Records. Mick Jagger even teamed up with Tosh for a duet of the Temptations' "(Got to Walk and) Don't Look Back." Jagger appeared with Tosh on *Saturday Night Live,* and Tosh's band Word, Sound, and Power toured with the Rolling Stones.

Tosh continued to return to the United States throughout the early eighties. He did two more albums for Rolling Stones Records, performed at London's Rainbow Theatre in 1981, and softened his sound with the single "Nothing But Love," a duet with Gwen Guthrie.

After releasing *Captured Live* and *No Nuclear War,* Tosh sought out Bunny Livingston, looking to reunite the Wailers. The two had already started to record when tragedy struck: on September 11, 1987, a burglar broke into Tosh's Jamaica home, and unfortunately, Tosh was in the house. He was brutally shot and killed in the botched burglary attempt. He was forty-two years old.

Heather O'Rourke

While eating at the MGM commissary, Heather O'Rourke was discovered at age five by director Steven Spielberg, who cast her as the lead in his 1982 movie, *Poltergeist.* She also appeared in several television shows, including the hit series *Happy Days,* on which

As was his nature, Peter Tosh took a more militant and revolutionary path after the breakup of the Wailers. His 1977 album, *Equal Rights,* cried out against racism and demanded that

blacks recognize their African homeland. During a 1978 Kingston concert, whose thirty thousand audience members included the Jamaican prime minister, Tosh smoked marijuana onstage

DEAD AT MGM

Rudolph Valentino (page 66) and Heather O'Rourke (page 63) are not the only MGM discoveries who met with early deaths.

Jean Harlow

Sensational blonde Jean Harlow took Hollywood by storm after Howard Hughes cast her in *Hell's Angels*, one of the first successful MGM talkies. She became one of the most popular actresses in Hollywood throughout the "Golden Years of MGM" in the early thirties, and weathered the

JEAN HARLOW POSES SEDUCTIVELY IN THIS UNDATED PUBLICITY PHOTO.

Irving Thalberg

Irving Thalberg was considered to be MGMs "boy genius" throughout the twenties and into the thirties. He paved the path for the studio's success, bringing a host of potential actors and actresses into the MGM fold, then packaging them into superstars—from his wife, Norma Shearer, to the dashing Clark Gable. Thalberg was responsible for such MGM successes as *The Big Parade* (1925), *Grand Hotel* (1932), and *A Night at the Opera* (1935). In stark contrast to his boss, Louis B. Mayer, Thalberg was also known as a kind and generous man. But in 1936, as he and Mayer began to go their separate ways, Thalberg died of pneumonia. He was thirty-seven. Today, the Academy of Motion Picture Arts and Sciences' Irving Thalberg Award honors lifetime achievement in the movie industry.

scandalous storm surrounding her husband Paul Bern's suicide in 1932. However, her life was cut horribly short when, at twenty-six, she died, like Valentino, of uremic poisoning. She was buried in a dress from her 1936 film, *Libeled Lady*.

Leslie Howard

Leslie Howard, who had worked with the studio for many years, was best known as Scarlett O'Hara's unattainable love, Ashley Wilkes, in the 1939 MGM classic *Gone With the Wind*. In 1943, Howard was on board a civilian plane from Lisbon to London, and the plane was shot down by the Germans over the Bay of Biscay. Everyone aboard, including fifty-three-year-old Howard, was killed.

ABOVE: LESLIE HOWARD AS ASHLEY WILKES WITH VIVIEN LEIGH AS SCARLETT O'HARA IN THE 1939 SCREEN CLASSIC *GONE WITH THE WIND*. RIGHT: IRVING THALBERG, HOLLYWOOD'S FIRST "BOY GENIUS," WAS RESPONSIBLE FOR MANY CLASSIC MGM MOVIES.

she played Heather Pfeiffer, the darling
little moppet who won Fonzie's heart.
O'Rourke went on to star in two
Poltergeist sequels in 1986 and 1987,
respectively.

On February 1, 1988, twelve-
year-old Heather complained of stomach pains, and was rushed to Children's
Hospital of San Diego, where doctors

discovered that the young girl had a
severe bowel obstruction. She was
rushed into surgery, but it was too late.
Her heart and lungs failed in surgery,
and she died.

Heather's fatal illness was determined the result of a congenital birth
defect. The obstruction had already led
to an infection that had spread, causing the septic shock that ultimately
killed her.

Heather O'Rourke's grave marker
reads, "Star of Poltergeist One, Two,
Three." She didn't have time to accom-
plish more.

Rudolph Valentino

Women loved him; men wanted to be
like him. Rudolph Valentino was an
enigmatic Hollywood creation, a real
man transformed into a fantasy.

Valentino came to America by
boat in steerage from his native Italy
at the age of eighteen. He headed to
Hollywood from New York after an
affair with a married woman turned
ugly (she shot and killed her husband—and her lawyer suggested that
Valentino quickly leave town). By
1921, he had scored his first starring
role, in MGM's *The Four Horsemen
of the Apocalypse*. The film propelled
him to instant stardom. He then did
another movie with MGM, when
actress Nazimova demanded he be
her love interest in *Camille*. After
a salary dispute, he left MGM and
moved to Paramount, where he
appeared in his most successful
role, as the Sheik in the movie of
the same name.

Perhaps because of his public
image, Valentino had deep personal

problems. His first wife, actress Jean
Acker, called their marriage a "horrible
mistake." His second wife was a domi-
nating woman, Natacha Rambova (née
Winifred Hudnut), a social climber
and set designer. The two married
before his divorce from Jean was complete and Valentino was charged with
bigamy. The couple had to swear that
the marriage hadn't been consummat-
ed—and live apart for a year. Once
they were living together, Natacha
took control of his life and career,
while he spent a fortune on her
to keep her happy—homes, cars,
antiques, and so on. Eventually, she
sued him for divorce, saying that he
was "too domesticated."

In addition to all this, while
Valentino was on his way to New
York to promote *The Son of the Sheik*
in 1926, the press released licentious
stories regarding his masculinity.
Valentino was rumored to be having
an affair with Ramon Novarro, another
"Latin lover" of the silver screen. As
if the yellow journalism wasn't bad
enough, when Valentino arrived in
New York, he was quite ill, suffering
from severe stomach pain.

On August 16, 1926, the thirty-
one-year-old Valentino collapsed in
his hotel room. He was taken to the
Polyclinic Hospital, the assumption
being that he had an ulcer. But
doctors found instead that his appen-
dix had burst and rushed him into
surgery. Unfortunately, it was too late:
uremic poisoning had swept through
his body, causing peritonitis and
septic endocarditis. On August 23
at 12:10 P.M., he died. His death
caused widespread hysteria. Women
fainted from grief, and more than
eighty thousand mourners trampled
one another to glimpse the corpse
of "The World's Greatest Lover."

AIDS AND THE ARTS

AIDS affects people in all walks of life. In the arts, this incurable killer virus has claimed so many lives that it has altered our cultural history. The following are just a few of its victims, struck down in the prime of their lives.

Brad Davis

Actor Brad Davis, who died in September 1991 at the age of forty-one, was best known for his portrayal of an American drug smuggler suffering the terror of imprisonment in Turkey in the 1978 motion picture *Midnight Express,* for which he won a Golden Globe Award.

ABOVE: BRAD DAVIS IN 1982'S *QUERELLE.* RIGHT: GRAFFITI VANDAL-TURNED-POP-ART SUPERSTAR KEITH HARING POSES WITH AN EXAMPLE OF HIS WORK.

Keith Haring

Pop artist Keith Haring was at one time the king of the Graffiti Kids who defaced Manhattan's subway walls in the early eighties. He soon became the rage of the New York art scene and later an international sensation. In February 1990, he died at the age of thirty-two.

John C. Holmes

Hardcore pornography star John C. Holmes' death sent shivers down the spine of an entire industry. Using the pseudonym Johnny Wadd, Holmes appeared in more than two thousand pornography films. He worked with all the top female stars, including Marilyn Chambers, Ginger Lynn, the underage Traci Lords, and the future Italian

parliament member Ciccolina (Ilona Staller). He was arrested thirteen times, mostly on indecency charges, but once for murder, of which he was acquitted. Holmes spent all of his seventy thousand dollars in savings on his medical care before he died in March 1988 at the age of forty-three.

Freddie Mercury

The flamboyant lead singer of the rock band Queen, Freddie Mercury used his operatic training and falsetto vocals to lead the group to huge success throughout the 1970s with songs like "Bohemian Rhapsody," "We Are the Champions," and "Killer Queen." Freddie Mercury was forty-four when he died in November 1991.

Ray Sharkey

Ray Sharkey won a Golden Globe Award in 1980 for *The Idolmaker*, in which he played a rock promoter based on real-life producer Bob Marcucci. Sharkey's mobster character on the television series *Wiseguy* was so popular that fans of the show formed the Sonny Steelgrave Memorial Society after the character was killed off. Sharkey died in June 1991 at forty.

ABOVE: FREDDIE MERCURY PERFORMING ONSTAGE IN ONE OF HIS TRADITIONALLY UNDERSTATED OUTFITS. HIS OPERATIC BACKGROUND AND SHOWY PERFORMANCE STYLE MADE QUEEN UNIQUE AMONG ROCK GROUPS.

Uncontrolled Substances

I could be the CATALYST that sparks the
*   revolution.*
I could be an INMATE in a long-term
*   institution*
I could lean to WILD extremes
*   I could do or DIE,*
I could yawn and be withdrawn
*   and watch them GALLOP by,*
What a waste, what a waste,
*   what a WASTE,*
*   what a waste.*

—Ian Drury, "What a Waste"

JOHN BELUSHI AS BLUTO IN *ANIMAL HOUSE*, THE TOP-GROSSING COMEDY OF 1978.

There is perhaps no method of celebrity demise more odious and yet more often repeated than that of the drug-related fatality. Despite the numerous sad examples of its consequences in the distant and more recent past, drug use continues today. Whether it is amphetamines, barbiturates, LSD, cocaine, heroin, or

BELOW: CATHY SMITH AT A COURT APPEARANCE. SHE WAS SENTENCED TO THREE YEARS IN PRISON FOR HER INVOLVEMENT IN JOHN BELUSHI'S DEATH. BOTTOM: THE BODY OF JOHN BELUSHI BEING CARRIED AWAY FROM THE CHATEAU MARMONT BUNGALOW IN WHICH HE DIED.

some insidious combination of these substances, the use of drugs has caused an astonishing number of deaths among young celebrities.

John Belushi

The year was 1982 and thirty-three-year-old John Belushi was in a career slump. Best known for portraying characters like the Samurai Warrior and the Cheeseburger Counterman on the NBC television show *Saturday Night Live*, as well as for his raunchy portrayal of a depraved fraternity boy in the 1978 hit movie *Animal House*, the hefty comedian was intent on becoming a serious actor. The movie studios, however, rejected his dramatic screenplay; one

of them even asked him to star in a wild comedy based on a sex manual instead. When he heard the news, a disgruntled Belushi left his wife in New York and flew to Los Angeles to meet with his studio contacts to discuss the matter.

Once he arrived in Los Angeles, he immediately resorted to the habit that for several years had been his antidote for stress—ingesting massive quantities of drugs. On March 4, his drug intake was staggering. Late in the day, Belushi met up with his friend Cathy Smith, a Gordon Lightfoot backup singer turned drug connection to the stars, at a friend's house. Smith provided the heroin, Belushi the cocaine. Smith mixed the two drugs and injected the concoction, known as a speedball, into both Belushi and herself several times. The pair moved on to another friend's house and shot up more speedballs. Later, at Belushi's favorite club, the Rox, they shot up again in the club's office. When the club closed, Belushi bought some more cocaine while sitting in his car in the parking lot and told all his buddies that the party would continue at the Chateau Marmont Hotel, where he had rented a bungalow. He then opened the car door and threw up on the pavement.

Robin Williams and Robert De Niro stopped by Belushi's Marmont bungalow that night, and both left shortly after seeing the scene: the room, littered with wine bottles and drug paraphernalia; the intoxicated Cathy Smith; and Belushi, himself, who drifted in and out of consciousness between snorts of cocaine. Once all the guests had left, Smith injected Belushi (who was complaining of being cold though the heat in the room was blasting) with one last speedball before he went to bed. Smith left in the morning to place a six-dollar bet on a horse.

LATE IN HIS CAREER, LENNY BRUCE CLAIMED THAT POLICE THREATENED TO ARREST ANY CLUB OWNER WHO ALLOWED HIM TO PERFORM.

Around noon on March 5, Belushi's physical trainer arrived at the party-trashed bungalow. He found the comedian in a fetal position under the bedcovers, pillow over his head. John Belushi was stone dead.

Lenny Bruce

Lenny Bruce, born in 1926, was heralded after his death as a martyr to the counterculture movement of the sixties. He earned his fame as the fast-talking purveyor of biting political and social commentary in the fifties. His scathing stand-up comedy spoken in bebop rhythm and peppered with profanities slung mud at the repression, conformity, and hypocrisy of the era, making him an underground hero to some and an anathema to many others, including the Catholic Church, the police, and Middle America. At the peak of his popularity, between 1960 and 1964, he was arrested nineteen times and was constantly barraged with frustrating, very costly legal battles involving obscenity and drug-related charges. He eventually became a crusader for freedom of speech and, after all his court trials, emerged nearly exonerated of all charges.

But he was much less than victorious in his personal life. He got too caught up in the fast lane of big-city nightlife, and his behavior became increasingly decadent. He did a lot of drugs, first becoming addicted to amphetamines and, later, heroin. He also indulged in spontaneous orgies. In 1965, he declared bankruptcy, due to his tremendous legal costs. In March of that year, naked and high on hallucinogens, Bruce somersaulted out of an upper-story window of a San Francisco hotel, nearly killing himself. He landed on his feet and broke both legs up to the hips.

After the plunge, he slowly began to lose his mind altogether. Paranoid and obsessed with his own mortality, he locked himself in his Hollywood Hills house and surrounded himself only by groupielike friends. He became flabby and sickly, injecting himself with more drugs to ease his physical and emotional pain.

On August 3, 1966, Bruce was found naked on the bathroom floor, where he had fallen from the toilet. There were fresh tracks in his scarred arm, and a bathrobe belt was tied around his bicep like a tourniquet. On the floor were drops of blood and the used needle. Lenny Bruce had died of a heroin overdose. He was forty years old.

Montgomery Clift

A handsome young man with a chiseled face and penetrating eyes, Montgomery Clift began his acting career in summer stock theater at twelve. He later moved on to the Broadway stage, where he was discovered by director Howard Hawks and cast opposite John Wayne in the 1948 motion picture *Red River*. Clift's early career was illustrious: he earned $100,000 per picture and was nominated for four Academy Awards. In 1953, he starred in his most memorable role as Pruitt, the peace-loving boxer–trumpet player in *From Here to Eternity*.

Clift's personal life, however, contrasted greatly with his professional success. Physically, he was weak; a problem with chronic diarrhea kept him from serving in World War II. Moreover, he suffered from severe emotional distress. Moody and sensitive, he was constantly in therapy trying to cope with his insecurities, his homosexuality, and his overprotective mother. But psychiatry did little to help Clift, so he soon began substituting drugs and alcohol for peace of mind. In fact, his Manhattan townhouse was equipped with an enormous medicine cabinet specially built to accommodate all his drugs. In 1954, Clift stopped acting altogether. He spent the next two years in seclusion with his self-doubts and mind-numbing intoxicants.

Eventually, Clift ran out of money and accepted a role in *Raintree County* (1957) opposite his good friend Elizabeth Taylor. On May 12, 1956, the actor attended a party at Taylor's estate. He left after dinner and, drunk and doped up, promptly wrapped his rental car around a telephone pole, shattering his face and crushing his nose and jaw, virtually transforming them into a shapeless mass of blood. When she arrived on the scene, Taylor yanked two teeth out of his throat, saving his life. But even after reconstructive surgery, his face was never the same and his good looks were forever lost.

After the accident, Clift's mental condition spiraled downhill. Although he still acted, doing roles in *Lonelyhearts* (1958), *Suddenly, Last Summer* (1959), *Wild River* (1960), *The Misfits* (1961), (opposite equally doomed stars Marilyn Monroe and Clark Gable), and *Judgment at Nuremberg* (1961), Clift mumbled through his lines and was disruptive on the set. At forty-five years old, Clift looked tired and worn. His physical health was failing and his drug problems were worse than ever. Taylor's insistence became the only reason anyone would hire Clift—she demanded he costar in her next movie, *Reflections in a Golden Eye* (1967).

Clift was in his New York townhouse with a friend on the night of July 22, 1966, just before filming was to begin. When the friend discovered that *The Misfits* was on television and asked if Clift wanted to watch, the actor replied, "Absolutely not!" Then he retired to his room.

Sometime during the night, after years of anguish and abuse, Montgomery Clift's heart stopped beating. He was found dead of a heart attack in the morning, lying naked on his bed, his troubled body and mind finally at rest.

MONTGOMERY CLIFT IN 1948. HIS DEVASTATING GOOD LOOKS BELIED HIS ANGUISHED PERSONALITY.

Brian Epstein

December 13, 1961, was a lucky day for Brian Epstein, a twenty-seven-year-old Liverpool record store manager, for it was the day he signed a contract to manage an impressive but unknown band he had seen gigging at the Cavern Club. The band was called the Beatles.

Epstein shaped the Beatles and with them carved out a huge slice of popular music history. He replaced drummer Pete Best with the effervescent Ringo Starr. He outfitted the rough-and-tumble foursome in neatly pressed designer suits and bowl haircuts, in effect creating a style of dress that was soon emulated the world over. He obtained a recording contract for the band with EMI/Parlaphone after Decca passed on the band, and it is rumored that he bought thousands of copies of the Beatles' first single, "Love Me Do," to help it hit the charts.

Epstein saw the Fab Four all the way from "I Wanna Hold Your Hand" to "A Day in the Life," from nowhere to megastardom. He furthered the Liverpool Sound by signing other talented acts, including Cilla Black, Gerry and the Pacemakers, and Billy J. Kramer and the Dakotas. He bought London's legendary West End theater, the Savile, and promoted a series of important mid-sixties rock concerts there. But his rock empire fell apart even as it grew, for the other acts never matched the Beatles' talent or success, and Epstein began to tire of managing the Fab Four. The thrill was gone, and Epstein struggled to keep up appearances as he delved into pill popping and promiscuity.

In 1967, in the process of turning the majority of his business dealings over to Robert Stigwood, manager of Jimi Hendrix, Cream, the Moody Blues, and the Bee Gees, Brian Epstein died of an accidental overdose of barbiturates. But his influence on popular music, embodied by the band he helped to create, is still alive today.

RAINER WERNER FASSBINDER WAS UNLUCKY IN LOVE: ONE OF HIS LOVERS DIED OF AN INTENTIONAL OVERDOSE; ANOTHER STABBED THREE PEOPLE AND LATER HANGED HIMSELF IN JAIL.

Rainer Werner Fassbinder

A legend among film students and aficionados the world over, German filmmaker Rainer Werner Fassbinder was born and raised in post–World War II West Germany. Between 1969 and 1982, he made forty-three art films, most of which he produced, wrote, and edited. He also acted and did camera work for many of them. With his brooding style and savagely dark perspective on social themes, as exempli-

fied in his most renowned work, *The Marriage of Maria Braun*, Fassbinder was an auteur in the truest sense of the word.

In his personal life, Fassbinder was an infamous carouser. No matter what he did, he did it to excess. He threw orgiastic two-day parties for moviedom's jet-setting A-list. He was promiscuous and sexually ambiguous (on the night of his wedding to Ingrid Caven, he had an affair with the best man), and enjoyed sadomasochistic adventures. He ate too much and drank too much, and had a predilection for the best champagne and Beluga caviar. As far as drugs were concerned, however, he wasn't as discriminating. He would snort as much as three grams of cocaine a day, mixing in heroin, nicotine from the cigarettes he chain-smoked, or virtually any other substance that was around. Then he'd take several Valium, along with ever-increasing doses of potent barbiturates, just in order to fall asleep at night.

By the age of thirty-seven, Fassbinder was obese, so worn and haggard that he barely had the energy to speak. On June 10, 1982, the abuse took its toll. Rainer Werner Fassbinder died in his sleep of a drug-related stroke.

Judy Garland

"That should have been the title of my life: 'Nobody Asked Me'." These were the words of one of the most cherished performers of all time, a woman whose voice exuded passion and pathos, harmony and joy—someone who will forever be a legend, Judy Garland.

From earliest childhood, Judy Garland (née Frances Ethel Gumm) had no control over her life. Her career was shaped by her overambitious stage moth-

er, a woman who would dominate Garland for most of her life. Garland never even saw her MGM contract, which allowed the studio to school her, to decide what roles she should do, and to alter her supposedly plain and pudgy demeanor.

It was four and a half years before Garland got her big break. Because Shirley Temple wasn't available, seventeen-year-old Garland catapulted to stardom as Dorothy in the 1939 classic *The Wizard of Oz*. To keep her looking as girlish as possible for the role, MGM put her on a strict diet that consisted of fasting, chicken broth, and a prescription of diet pills (amphetamines). In this way, she was able to get through the rigorous filming schedule of *The Wizard of Oz* without eating.

JUDY GARLAND AS DOROTHY AND RAY BOLGER AS THE SCARECROW IN *THE WIZARD OF OZ* (1939).

In the next six years that followed, Garland was making films at a breakneck pace, primarily with costar Mickey Rooney. She entered the first of five unsuccessful marriages (she was married to David Rose, Vincent Minnelli, Sid Luft, Mark Herron, and Mickey Deans) and, most significantly, began smoking heavily and riding a roller coaster of alcohol and drug abuse. When her amphetamine-laced diet pills and the hectic pace of moviemaking kept her awake at night, the studio provided her with barbiturates to help her sleep. When she tried early on to get psychiatric help, both her mother and the studio fiercely objected, fearing that a strong and sane "property" would be difficult to control. By 1950, after performing in such memorable movies as *Meet Me in St. Louis* and *Easter Parade*, she was so emotionally distraught, unstable, temperamental, and suicidal that the studio finally sent her off for a "rest cure"—but the damage was irreparable.

Just months after she was released from treatment, she slit her throat with a piece of glass on June 20, 1950. The unsuccessful suicide attempt served to escalate her personal and professional turmoils. Her husband at the time, film-director Vincent Minnelli, promptly divorced her, and MGM, the studio for which she had made millions, dropped her. In 1952, her mother, whom Garland had once referred to as "the real-life Wicked Witch of the West," died, and for the first time in her life, Garland was free to make her own decisions. She married for the third time, to movie producer Sid Luft, later that year.

The ensuing years were initially successful for Garland. She dazzled audiences in live performances, including a Carnegie Hall appearance in 1961, and won an Academy Award nomination for the 1954 remake of *A Star Is Born*.

THE YELLOW BRICK ROAD LED TO RUIN FOR GARLAND WHO, LATE IN HER SHORT LIFE, WAS EVICTED FROM THE ST. MORITZ HOTEL BECAUSE SHE COULDN'T PAY HER ROOM BILL.

But the sixties were indeed Garland's saddest years. Her weekly television series, *The Judy Garland Show* (1963–1964), a variety show in which she often appeared drunk, was canceled after one year. Her marriage to Luft ended with a divorce and a bitter custody war. Although she was brilliant in *Judgment at Nuremberg*, she was fired from several other movies. She moved from hotel to hotel, usually one step ahead of rent collectors, and was constantly in and out of hospitals because of drug- or alcohol-related illness. By 1969, she was on her fifth marriage, to sometime-nightclub performer, sometime-waiter Mickey Deans. She was performing on stage again, in London, but her voice was shot; she would talk her way through her shows, often slurring her words. She was forty-seven years old, but her body and face were ravaged by years of abuse; she looked much older.

On June 22, 1969, Deans awoke at 11 A.M. in response to a phone call from a friend in England. Deans had last seen his wife around midnight the night before when, ill with strep throat, she had taken a dose of sleeping pills before bed. Since Garland was not in the bedroom he searched the apartment and found the bathroom door locked. He pounded on the door and, receiving no response, managed to climb onto the roof and look in through the window. Garland was sitting on the toilet, slumped over dead.

It is thought that sometime in the early morning, Garland had taken another dose of sleeping pills. An autopsy revealed that she had ingested one barbiturate too many and simply had ceased to breathe. Despite speculations of suicide, the coroner called Garland's death an accidental overdose.

Billie Holiday

Elenora Gough's mother said of her daughter, "She used to annoy an aunt with how she was living by sing-ing...blues about 'my man this and my man that'" when the girl was just eight years old. But Elenora became the greatest singer of her time and one of the greatest jazz singers ever, Billie Holiday.

Abandoned by her father, abused and raped as a child, Holiday spent her teens working in private clubs in Baltimore as a singer and occasional prostitute. By the mid-thirties, Holiday had moved to New York and was singing with some of the era's great musicians: Johnny Hodges, Buck Clayton, and Lester Young. In 1935, she premiered at the Apollo Theater

ABOVE: A 1938 PORTRAIT OF BILLIE HOLIDAY. THE SWATCH OF GARDENIAS IN HER HAIR BECAME A TRADEMARK. LEFT: FRIENDS AND FANS LINE THE STREET AS HOLIDAY'S CASKET IS CAR-RIED INTO A NEW YORK CHURCH ON JULY 21, 1959.

----

in Harlem and was offered a recording contract with Columbia Records, with whom she recorded what became her theme song, "Them There Eyes." She sang with Count Basie's band in 1937 and with that of Artie Shaw in 1938.

By the mid-forties, "Lady Day" was a star. She sang with every musician of note, and her hits for Decca Records, "Billie's Blues" (1936), "Strange Fruit" (1939), and "Lover Man" (1944), made her the most famous jazz singer of her

day. Her career peaked in the early fifties, when she played Carnegie Hall.

Holiday's personal life is just as legendary as her talent. Her abuse at the hands of the many men in her life, her stormy marriage to Louis McKay (who later acted as a consultant to the film *Lady Sings the Blues*, 1972), her many arrests on drug charges, and her addiction to heroin made for tabloid sensation, and a life cut short.

Comedian Steve Allen remembers seeing Holiday before a performance at the Phoenix Theater in 1959: he described her as "skinny as a rail—looking like someone you see in pic-

tures out of Dachau." Later that year, she was admitted to New York's Metropolitan Hospital after collapsing at

home. She continued to sniff heroin while in the hospital until a nurse found a tinfoil packet of the drug in her room. Holiday was arrested in her hospital bed on June 12, 1959. But she died a little over a month later, on July 17, before she could serve time in jail, at forty-four.

Anissa Jones

Anissa Jones is remembered as Buffy, the sweet-faced little moppet who wore starched crinoline dresses, her curly blonde hair in pigtails, on the popular sixties television series *Family Affair*, which still runs in syndication today.

In reality, Jones, who was already eight years old in 1966 when the series began, hated the puffy doll-like "baby clothes" she was forced to wear. In fact, she didn't particularly want to be in show business at all. She wanted to be at school with her friends, living a normal life. But her divorced mother was intent on making her a star. Jones played Buffy for five years.

When *Family Affair* went off the air in 1971, Jones was thirteen, trying to be a normal teenager despite her lost childhood. But she couldn't make the transition and turned to drugs and alcohol in a desperate attempt to cope with life outside of television stardom. It wasn't long before lovable Buffy was a drug addict.

On August 29, 1976, eighteen-year-old Jones was staying at a girlfriend's house, downing alcohol mixed with Quaaludes. The mixture proved lethal, for the former child star was found dead on the floor where she had landed in a heap sometime during the night.

Charlie Parker

Charlie Parker was perhaps the greatest figure in jazz history. The saxophonist was a musical genius who aspired to translate everything he saw into musical beauty. Not only was he the father of bebop—the precursor to modern, or "cool," jazz—Parker, nicknamed "Yardbird" or "Bird," inspired countless musicians who played with him and came after him, including Miles Davis, Dizzy Gillespie, Thelonious Monk, and Max Roach. Among Parker's many legendary songs are "Bird of Paradise" (1946), "Yardbird Suite" (1946), and "Relaxin' at Camarillo" (1947), which was written while he was hospitalized at Camarillo State Hospital in California after a nervous breakdown.

An alcoholic and a heroin addict, Parker was a gallivanter who married many times and had many girlfriends. He would just as soon walk off the stage before a paying crowd than play when he didn't feel like it. He sometimes stunned audiences by playing one tune while his string band played another. In 1954, he attempted suicide twice, the first time by swallowing iodine.

Parker's last performance was on March 5, 1955, at Birdland, the club that was named after him. He died at the age of thirty-four when, after years of narcotics abuse, his stomach, liver, and heart failed him. In fact, his body

THE YARDBIRD, CHARLIE PARKER. AFTER HE DIED, FANS WROTE THE WORDS "BIRD LIVES" ON THE WALLS OF JAZZ CLUBS FROM NEW YORK TO PARIS.

----

was in such poor condition that the doctor who performed the autopsy on him thought that Parker was more than fifty years old.

River Phoenix

At twenty-three, River Phoenix was already a star. He had performed to critical acclaim in numerous movies including *Stand by Me* (1986), *Mosquito Coast* (1986), and *Running on Empty* (1988), the last of which won him an Academy Award nomination. He was smart, handsome, and charming, and he loved to party, experimenting with various mixtures of drugs and alcohol in search of the perfect high. He frequented the hippest Hollywood clubs, surrounded by an entourage of successful young actors and musicians like Keanu Reeves, Christian Slater, and R.E.M.'s Michael Stipe. Despite his substance abuse, he was a serious vegetarian and diligent about keeping in shape. But it wasn't enough.

On October 30, 1993, Phoenix had on hand all the necessary ingredients for another night of debauchery. The

CLASSIC DEAD

Artist	**Duane Allman**	**John Bonham**	**Lowell George**	**Jimi Hendrix**	
Band	Allman Brothers Band	Led Zeppelin	Little Feat	Jimi Hendrix Experience	
Hit Song	"Revival (Love Is Everywhere)"	"Whole Lotta Love"	"Long Distance Love"	"Purple Haze"	
Instrument	Guitar	Bass guitar	Guitar	Guitar	
Drug(s) of Choice	Marijuana	Alcohol	Amphetamines	LSD, barbiturates	
Where Died	Highway, Macon, Georgia	His home, London	Motel, Arlington, Virginia	His apartment, London	
Age	24	32	34	27	
Date	October 29, 1971	September 25, 1980	June 6, 1979	September 18, 1970	
Cause of Death	Motorcycle crash	Choked in sleep after heavy drinking	Heart attack brought on by drug abuse	Inhalation of vomit due to barbiturate intoxication	

> *"Fourteen heart attacks and he had to die in my week. In MY week."*
>
> —Janis Joplin (when Dwight D. Eisenhower's death prevented her photograph from being on the cover of *Newsweek*)

Brian Jones	Janis Joplin	Keith Moon	Jim Morrison	Bon Scott
Rolling Stones	Big Brother & the Holding Company	The Who	The Doors	AC/DC
"Satisfaction"	"Me 'n Bobby McGee"	"Who Are You"	"Light My Fire"	"Highway to Hell"
Guitar	Voice	Drums	Voice	Voice
Amphetamines	Heroin	Alcohol	Alcohol, LSD	Alcohol
His swimming pool, Cotchford Farm, England	Landmark Hotel, Hollywood, California	His Part Street apartment, London (same building where Cass Elliot died)	Bathtub of his apartment, Paris, France	Alistair Kennear's car, South London
28	27	31	28	33
July 3, 1969	October 4, 1970	September 8, 1978	July 3, 1971	February 2, 1980
Drowned (large quantity of unknown drug found in system)	Heroin overdose	Overdose of Heminevrin, a drug prescribed to combat alcoholism	Overdose (drug of unknown origin)	Drank himself to death

evening began in room 328 of the posh Hotel Nikko in West Hollywood, where, with a group of friends, he began to ingest a combination of drugs, wine, and hard liquor. At 10 P.M., when a hotel waiter arrived to deliver dinner, Phoenix, his eyes dazed and bloodshot, was dancing in circles in the middle of the room. At about 10:30, the party moved to Johnny Depp's swank Sunset

LEFT: ACTOR RIVER PHOENIX RECEIVED AN OSCAR NOMINATION WHEN HE WAS ONLY SEVENTEEN YEARS OLD. BELOW: FANS PAY HOMAGE TO PHOENIX ON THE SIDEWALK OUTSIDE THE VIPER ROOM, WHERE THE ACTOR COLLAPSED AND DIED.

Strip club, the Viper Room. That night Depp was onstage jamming with Michael Balzary (Flea of the rock group Red Hot Chili Peppers). Television and film actress Christina Applegate was also there.

At the club, River met up with his girlfriend, actress and former costar Samantha Mathis, his brother, Joaquin, and his sister, Rainbow. He also continued his binge, although he could barely form the words necessary to order anything. He and his friends began to drink shots of the potent German drink Jägermeister. Soon, Phoenix vomited on himself, then briefly passed out. He had been spotted in the men's room having convulsions, yet none of his friends thought it necessary to do anything about his condition until it was too late.

When Mathis finally helped him outside the club, he collapsed on the sidewalk and began to convulse violently, his hands and head uncontrollably pounding the pavement. According to a witness, Mathis and Joaquin argued with the club's doorman as River writhed on the ground. Finally, Rainbow jumped on his stricken body to try to stop the seizures while a frantic Joaquin called for emergency help. But by the time the paramedics arrived, Phoenix was in full cardiac arrest.

Although the doctors went so far as to insert a pacemaker to stimulate his heart, it was no use. River Phoenix was pronounced dead at 1:51 A.M. on October 31, 1993.

Shortly after, the police searched River's hotel room. They found empty liquor bottles and Valium, as well as heroin and cocaine.

Elvis Presley

Perhaps the most shocking and celebrated music-related drug tragedy is that of Elvis Presley. The first rock superstar, Elvis was a drug addict of epic proportions. Prescription drugs—amphetamines, barbiturates, painkillers, and tranquilizers—all contributed

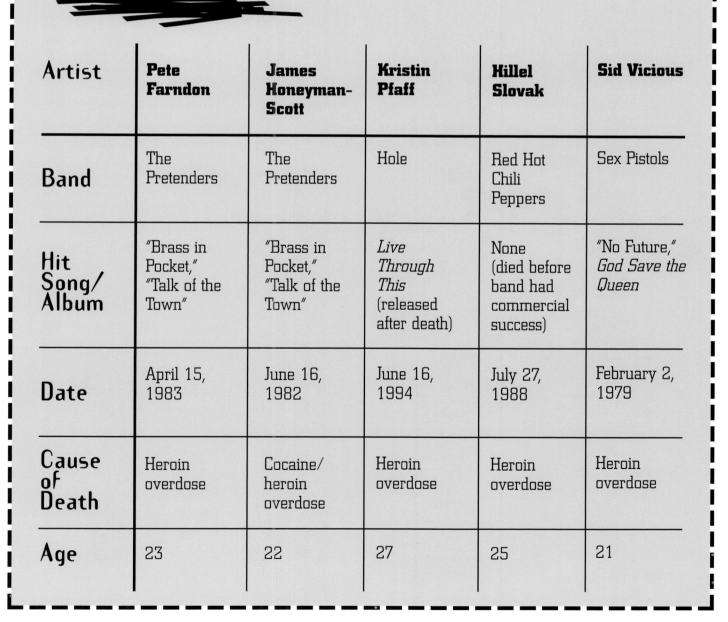

NEW WAVE/ ALTERNATIVE DEAD

Artist	Pete Farndon	James Honeyman-Scott	Kristin Pfaff	Hillel Slovak	Sid Vicious
Band	The Pretenders	The Pretenders	Hole	Red Hot Chili Peppers	Sex Pistols
Hit Song/ Album	"Brass in Pocket," "Talk of the Town"	"Brass in Pocket," "Talk of the Town"	*Live Through This* (released after death)	None (died before band had commercial success)	"No Future," *God Save the Queen*
Date	April 15, 1983	June 16, 1982	June 16, 1994	July 27, 1988	February 2, 1979
Cause of Death	Heroin overdose	Cocaine/ heroin overdose	Heroin overdose	Heroin overdose	Heroin overdose
Age	23	22	27	25	21

to Elvis' downfall. Drugs, combined with a penchant for food and numerous health problems (including digestive problems and hypertension) for which he took more drugs, transformed the handsome, svelte, sexy, talented Elvis of fifties' fame into a flabby parody of himself by the seventies. In the seven months before his death, Presley's doctor allegedly prescribed a total of fifty-three hundred pills and vials for him.

On August 16, 1977, while reading a book entitled *The Scientific Search for the Face of Jesus* as he sat on the toilet in the bathroom of his Graceland mansion, Presley fell to the floor. He was rushed to a Memphis hospital, where he was pronounced dead an hour later. The autopsy revealed an enlarged liver and advanced arteriosclerosis. The coroner ruled death by natural causes, but Elvis' death was hardly natural; some years later, it was revealed that he died of the cumulative effects of taking many different medications in combination and at high dosages for quite some time.

Thousands of fans gathered at Graceland, Elvis' estate in Memphis, to mourn his passing. In the years after his death, Elvis became an icon of god-like stature, a religion to his die-hard fans. Those thousands of fans continue to remember Elvis Presley today, commemorating his death each year with candlelight vigils, and continuing to appreciate his true contribution—his timeless music and voice.

BY THE EARLY SEVENTIES, ELVIS PRESLEY WAS DOING SO MANY DRUGS THAT WHEN HE WENT ONSTAGE HE OFTEN COULDN'T REMEMBER THE LYRICS TO HIS OWN SONGS.

Hank Williams

Country music lost its first superstar to substance abuse. Hank Williams was responsible for classic hits like "Your Cheating Heart" (1952) and "Hey, Good Lookin'" (1951). He was also the first country star to cross over to the pop charts. But his stay at the top lasted only four years.

Born in Macedonia, Alabama, in 1923, Williams spent much of his boyhood living in a boxcar and hawking peanuts on the streets of Montgomery. He later turned that skill into performing as a street musician. He also started drinking when he was eleven.

By the time he was seventeen, Williams was performing on local radio stations and winning local talent contests. In January 1947, Williams' first record was released by an obscure record label, Sterling, to modest success. In June, now with MGM, Williams released "Move It on Over." By 1948, he was starring on the famous *Louisiana Hayride* radio show, and in 1949 he released "Lovesick Blues," which went to number one on the *Billboard* country charts.

Despite his enormous talent and success, Williams' personal life was a disaster. His first marriage, to Audrey Guy, fell apart because of his heavy

ABOVE, RIGHT: HANK WILLIAMS AND HIS FIRST WIFE, AUDREY GUY, THEIR SON, HANK WILLIAMS, JR., AND GUY'S DAUGHTER FROM ANOTHER MARRIAGE, LUCRETIA. THE SONG *COLD, COLD HEART* WAS REPORTEDLY INSPIRED BY HANK AND AUDREY'S TUMULTUOUS RELATIONSHIP.

drinking, womanizing, and abusive behavior, as well as Audrey's aspirations for success as a singer, despite an obvious lack of talent. In addition, Williams' chronic back pain furthered his substance abuse, as he became addicted to painkillers—and that was long before he began to miss gigs and arrive drunk for his dates at the Grand Old Opry.

On December 31, 1952, the twenty-nine-year-old country superstar was en route to a show in Canton, Ohio. His driver, eighteen-year-old Charles Carr, stopped at a hotel in Knoxville, Tennessee, because Williams had passed out in the car, and Carr asked for a doctor to be called. Two porters carried the unconscious Williams to his room. When

a doctor arrived, he administered two shots of morphine mixed with vitamin B12 to Williams. The next day, porters carried a seemingly lifeless Williams o the car, and Carr and Williams proceeded on their way to Ohio.

Outside of Rutledge, Tennessee, Carr was stopped for speeding. The patrolman looked at Williams and asked, "He's not dead, is he?" Carr followed the patrolman into Rutledge, where he was fined for speeding. Despite Williams' condition, the driver was allowed to continue on his way. But by the time Carr reached Oakville, Virginia, he determined that something was really wrong with Williams and drove to a local hospital, where Williams was pronounced dead.

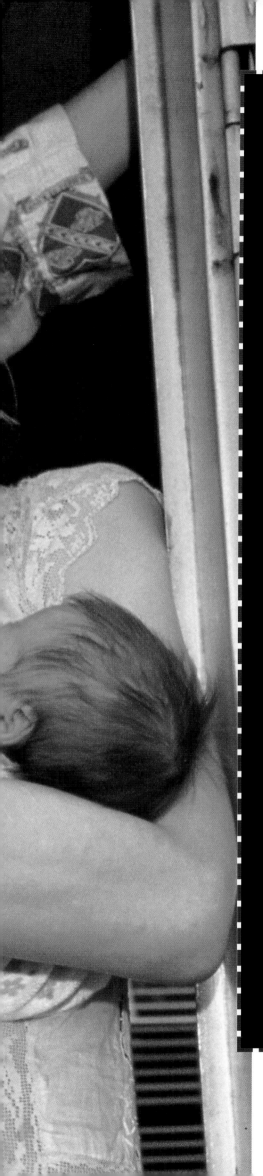

CHAPTER FIVE

Suicide Is Painless

RÉSUMÉ

RAZORS pain you;

Rivers are damp;

Acids STAIN you;

And drugs cause cramp.

GUNS aren't lawful;

Nooses give;

Gas smells awful;

You might as well LIVE.

—Dorothy Parker

KURT COBAIN WITH HIS WIFE, COURTNEY LOVE, AND THEIR
DAUGHTER, FRANCES BEAN COBAIN.

Sometimes, a creative outlet is the only salvation of an otherwise disturbed personality. And sometimes, the pressures of fame, even for the well-adjusted, can become burdensome beyond tolerance. It is not surprising—though not any less tragic—when artists take their own lives as a result of personal problems or the pressure of being in the public eye, or both.

Kurt Cobain

Kurt Cobain was labeled a spokesman for his generation, a title he wore like a noose. Cobain, with his band Nirvana, became the archetype for the Seattle "grunge sound," popularized alternative music, and brought a new attitude to rock music in the nineties. But Cobain was also an intense loner who shunned the spotlight, which shone glaringly upon him. He became Generation X's first casualty.

Cobain was born on February 20, 1967, and raised in a trailer park in Aberdeen, Washington, a lumber town long past its prime. As a child, he didn't fit in with the roughneck kids who tormented him, so he turned to music, writing songs and playing drums and, later, guitar.

After dropping out of high school, he met Krist Novoselic. Personally and musically, the two hit it off. "I lived with Kurt for eight months," Novoselic remembered. "He had just broken up with a girl and was totally heartbroken. We would sit in his tiny shoe-box apartment for eight hours at a time without saying a word. Finally one night, we were driving in the van and Kurt said, 'You know, I'm not always like this.'" A Beatles fan, Cobain would later say that "[John] Lennon was obviously disturbed. So I could relate to

that." Cobain and Novoselic went through several incarnations as a garage band: Skid Row, Fecal Matter, and finally Nirvana. With the addition of drummer Dave Grohl, Cobain finally found a winning combination.

In 1989 Sub-Pop, a tiny alternative record label, released Nirvana's first record *Bleach*, reportedly recorded for only six hundred dollars. The album received critical praise from several underground publications, and it sold more than thirty thousand copies. A year and a half of small gigs followed, during which the band honed its performing skills. Meanwhile, Cobain, who had written a new collection of songs for Nirvana's next album, began shopping his group to major record labels. The group landed a major recording contract with MCA Records, an industry giant. Nirvana's second record, *Nevermind* (1992), changed the course of rock and roll. Its signature song, "Smells Like Teen Spirit," was adopted by a disaffected generation as an anthem of discontent and cynicism. The album went to the Top Ten, "grunge" became a part of the national vocabulary, and the record industry invaded Seattle's rock scene in hope of finding another Nirvana.

As the band's fame skyrocketed, Cobain's personal life became even more of a roller coaster. He was plagued by a chronic stomach condition that caused him a tremendous amount of pain, which he tried to exorcise through the wildly raucous shows Nirvana played on tour and by "medicating himself" with heroin. His marriage in 1991 to Courtney Love, the brash leader of the punk group Hole, seemed to bring him some security, comfort, and, perhaps for the first time in his life, someone who understood him. In 1992, the couple had a daugh-

ter, Frances Bean. But rumors of the couple's drug abuse ran rampant, and a notorious *Vanity Fair* article that same year accused Love of using heroin while she was pregnant, a charge she adamantly denies. Nevertheless, child and welfare authorities took the charge seriously and Love and Cobain were not allowed to be alone with their baby for one month.

Cobain's drug use continued to be a problem. In May 1993, Love summoned police after Cobain overdosed on heroin. In June, police arrested Cobain for domestic assault; a large assortment of guns was confiscated from the couple's home. In 1994, while on tour in Europe, Cobain overdosed again but was taken to a hospital in Rome, where he lay in a coma for twenty hours. Despite the suicide note Cobain had written, the couple afterward called the overdose "an accident." Cobain recovered and he, Love, and Frances returned to Seattle. But things didn't get any better.

On March 18, 1994, Love again called police to the couple's Seattle home, where several guns, twenty-five boxes of ammunition, and drugs were confiscated. After the incident, Love, Cobain's friends, and band mates staged an "intervention," trying to convince Cobain that his drug use was killing him. At the end of March Cobain and Love both went to Los Angeles, where he checked into a drug rehabilitation clinic while she put some finishing touches on an upcoming album. From the clinic, Cobain placed a call to

COBAIN, LOVE, AND FRANCES BEAN AT THE MTV MUSIC VIDEO AWARDS IN 1993.

his wife, saying, "Just remember, no matter what, I love you."

Shortly thereafter, Cobain snuck out of the drug clinic and headed back to Seattle. A few days later, on April 3, his mother filed a missing persons report with the police. On April 5, Cobain barricaded himself inside a room above the couple's garage. He placed his wallet on the floor, open to his driver's license (presumably to help police identify him), injected some heroin, placed the barrel of a shotgun to his forehead, and pulled the trigger. He lay there for two and a half days before his body was discovered by an electrician working on the house.

Meanwhile, on April 7, Love was taken to a Los Angeles hospital, where she was treated for a drug overdose. Upon her discharge, police charged her with possession of both a controlled substance and drug paraphernalia, and possession of/receiving stolen property. After posting bail, she checked into the same rehabilitation center her husband had escaped from one week earlier. But she checked out the next day, when she received news of her husband's suicide.

NIRVANA: DAVE GROHL, KURT COBAIN, AND KRIST NOVOSELIC. THE BAND DEFINED ROCK AND ROLL IN THE NINETIES.

On April 10, several thousand fans gathered at a park near the Seattle Space Needle for a candlelight vigil, where a taped message was broadcast: Love's reading of Cobain's suicide note. At the same time, Cobain's family and friends held a service for 150 mourners. After the service ended, Love joined the public vigil, where, still clutching her dead husband's suicide note, she handed out some of his old clothes and possessions.

A week later, Hole's second album, ironically titled *Live Through This,* was released, propelling Courtney Love to superstardom. (Two months later, Kristin Pfaff, the bassist for Courtney Love's band, died of a heroin overdose.)

HANGINGS

Soon after Kurt Cobain's suicide, **Doug Hopkins**, guitarist and songwriter for the popular alternative band the Gin Blossoms, also killed himself with a gun. Prior to Hopkins' death, the method of choice for suicidal musicians who didn't overdose seemed to be hanging themselves.

After a run of hits in the early seventies, including "Day After Day," "No Matter What," and "Baby Blue," **Peter Ham**'s band, Badfinger, was faltering. After two album flops and internal dissension, the band lost its record contract. Already suffering from personal problems, twenty-seven-year-old Pete Ham became deeply depressed. He hanged himself in 1975. Ham's suicide was followed by that of **Phil Ochs**, the sixties protest singer-songwriter whose "I Ain't Marching" was an anti–Vietnam War anthem. In 1973, Ochs was nearly strangled to death while traveling in Africa. The mysterious attack permanently damaged his vocal cords and intensified the depression he had suffered from for years. In 1976, at the age of thirty-five, he hanged himself at his sister's house. At about the same time, the Band, responsible for several classic rock songs, such as "The Weight" and "Up on Cripple Creek," broke up. After the

breakup, all of the Band's members moved on to new ventures—all except pianist-vocalist **Richard Manuel**. He hanged himself ten years later at forty-one. Finally, the post-punk Manchester, England, band Joy Division garnered rave reviews in 1980 for their debut album, *Unknown Pleasures*. But later that year, the lead singer, twenty-three-year-old **Ian Curtis**, hanged himself just before the band was supposed to go onstage. Curtis, whose gloomy and morbid lyrics were the benchmarks of the band's success, had long suffered from epilepsy and severe depression. After his suicide, Joy Division became New Order, adopted a lighter sound, and, in 1983, produced the top-selling *Blue Monday*. The band continues to perform today.

ABOVE: IAN CURTIS OF JOY DIVISION. LEFT: PETER HAM (SINGING) PERFORMING WITH BADFINGER.

Peg Entwistle

Peg Entwistle, a blonde, blue-eyed native of London, England, was already a semisuccessful Broadway stage actress when she decided to try her luck in the movies. She arrived in Hollywood in 1932, was cast in a short-lived play, then scored her first motion picture, *Thirteen Women* (1932), with Myrna Loy.

But *Thirteen Women* was so bad that the studio demanded it be recut before its release. Then RKO terminated Entwistle's contract. Completely despondent, she tried to borrow enough money for train fare back to New York, but was denied the loan.

After eating dinner on September 18, 1932, Entwistle put on a nice dress she had borrowed from an actress friend and walked to a huge lightbulb-studded sign in the Hollywood Hills advertising a land development, "HOLLYWOODLAND." (The last four letters fell off the sign as a result of a mudslide during World War II.) She stopped below the H, took off her jacket

PEG ENTWHISTLE (SEATED, RIGHT) AND THE CAST OF *THIRTEEN WOMEN*, HER ONLY FILM.

----

and placed it neatly on the ground next to her purse, then proceeded to climb an electrician's ladder fifty feet (15m) to the top of the sign, losing one of her shoes along the way. Once she reached the top, she jumped to her death. Her twisted corpse lay there for several days before it was found, but when it was, along with the accompanying suicide note, it made quite a stir. The actress was the first person ever to jump from the sign, and the act was fraught with symbolism for Hollywood's critics and rejects. In fact, Entwistle's act was repeated enough times that the sign was eventually cut off from public access. In her own way, Peg Entwistle had finally become famous.

WRITER SYLVIA PLATH WON THE
PULITZER PRIZE IN POETRY FOR
ARIEL, A POSTHUMOUS COLLECTION
OF HER WORK, NINE YEARS AFTER
SHE KILLED HERSELF.

Sylvia Plath

"Stop thinking selfishly of razors and self-wounds and going out and ending it all. Your room is not your prison. You are."

Sylvia Plath wrote these words in the summer following her junior year at Smith College. Shortly afterward, her mother, concerned over Sylvia's mounting depression, took her daughter to a psychiatrist, who prescribed shock treatments. The electroconvulsive shocks proved painful and horrifying to the brilliant twenty-year-old writer. On August 24, 1953, several days after one of the treatments, Plath hid in a crawl space under a bedroom in her mother's house and swallowed a nearly full bottle of sleeping pills. After an intensive two-day search, she was found—barely alive.

Plath survived her first suicide attempt and went on to study in England at Cambridge University in 1955, where she met her future husband, poet Ted Hughes. They married a year later and returned to Massachusetts, where their two children were born in 1960 and 1962. Plath published *The Colossus* in 1960.

In 1963, Plath was gaining recognition as a poet. Moreover, her book *The Bell Jar* had been published to favorable reviews. Her personal life, however, was not so positive. She still suffered from acute depression, and bouts with a severe flu had left her thin, frail, and sickly. But it was the heart-wrenching collapse of her troubled marriage to the philandering Hughes that finally drove her over the edge.

Early in the morning on February 11, 1963, Plath left cups of milk next to the beds of her two children. She barricaded herself in the kitchen, lodging towels under and taping the crevices around the doors. After ingesting a large quantity of sleeping pills, she wrote a note asking her nurse, who was to arrive later that morning, to call her doctor. Then she knelt beside the oven and turned on the gas. When her nurse arrived at 9:30 A.M., thirty-year-old Sylvia Plath was dead.

Since Plath's divorce from Hughes was never finalized, he won control of the literary rights to all of his wife's works. Soon after Plath died, he chose and edited a collection of her later poems, *Ariel*, for publication. In 1982, the Hughes-edited *Sylvia Plath, Collected Works* won the Pulitzer Prize for poetry.

WRITER'S BLOCK

Author	Hart Crane	Jerzy Kosinski	Anne Sexton	Virginia Woolf
Famous Work	*The Bridge*	*Being There*	*Live or Die*	*A Room of One's Own*
Method of Suicide	Jumped from a steamer en route from Mexico to New York	Suffocated himself due to physical health problems. He was found in half-full bathtub with plastic bag over his head	Sat in her 1967 Mercury Cougar in a closed garage, where she died from carbon monoxide poisoning	Put rocks in her pockets and drowned herself in the Ouse River. Her body was found three weeks later
Date	April 27, 1932	May 3, 1991	October 4, 1974	March 28, 1941
Times Tried	1	1	7	2
Notes	His body was never found.	If not for losing his luggage in Paris, he would have been in Roman Polanski's house the night Sharon Tate and friends were murdered there.	She used to compare suicide attempts with Sylvia Plath.	Her first suicide attempt was thirty-seven years before her second.

Freddie Prinze

As a teenager, Freddie Prinze almost overdosed on Valium when the pressure of Manhattan's competitive High School of Performing Arts became too intense for him to bear. He was no stranger to drugs and used Valium, cocaine, and marijuana to quell his insecurities, yet the Hungarian–Puerto Rican comedian from one of New York City's worst neighborhoods managed to live through high school. Soon after, Prinze began performing stand-up comedy at Manhattan's Improv comedy club. In 1973, at the age of nineteen, Prinze performed his act on *The Tonight Show* with Johnny Carson. A television producer saw Prinze's performance and cast him opposite Jack Albertson in the television series *Chico and the Man*.

Prinze and the series became a huge success in a very short time. By 1976, he was a millionaire living in Los Angeles with a wife and son, and he was adored by throngs of fans everywhere. But he also increased his use of drugs—cocaine and Quaaludes—washing them down with wine. Eventually, the pressure of being a star was too much for him to bear. He began taking more intoxicants, ingesting as many as one hundred Quaaludes each day. He was also arrested for driving under the influence of drugs and alcohol. By the end of 1976, his wife could no longer tolerate the situation and petitioned for a divorce.

In January 1977, Prinze was living in a plush hotel room in Los Angeles while adhering to a rigorous shooting schedule for his television series, performing his stand-up routine, as well as taking karate classes and going to ther-apy to relieve the strain. But nothing seemed to help except Quaaludes. Prinze also began to tell friends that "life isn't worth living." He would then hold a gun to his head and jokingly pull the trigger.

In the early morning of January 29, Prinze's manager, Martin "Dusty" Snyder, received a disturbing phone call from his client, then hurried over to Prinze's hotel room. When Snyder arrived, Prinze, dressed in his karate pants, smiled and handed his manager a note that read, "I cannot go on any longer." Prinze proceeded to call his estranged wife, his attorney, his secretary, and his mother, no doubt conveying the same message. Meanwhile, Snyder went into another room and called Prinze's therapist, who assured the panicked manager that his client was only "crying out for attention."

FREDDIE PRINZE (RIGHT) AS CHICO, WITH TELEVISION COSTAR JACK ALBERTSON IN *CHICO AND THE MAN*.

Snyder went back to Prinze, who was sitting on the sofa where, moments later, the star took out a .38 revolver from under a pillow and held it to his head. Snyder lunged, but Prinze waved the gun back at him. Snyder kept his distance, trying desperately to talk the young actor out of taking his own life. Freddie held the revolver loosely by his side, staring blankly at Snyder for a long moment, then swept the gun up to his temple and fired. He fell back onto the sofa, blood spewing from his temple. Twenty-two-year-old Freddie Prinze lived, brain-dead, for thirty-seven hours before he expired.

After a court battle, Prinze's mother convinced a judge that her son had been acting under the influence of drugs and had not intended to take his own life, thereby winning a hefty insurance settlement for Prinze's ex-wife and son. But what most likely happened to Freddie Prinze was that he finally collapsed under the enormous pressure of his own success, completing with his suicide the self-destructive cycle he had been on since high school.

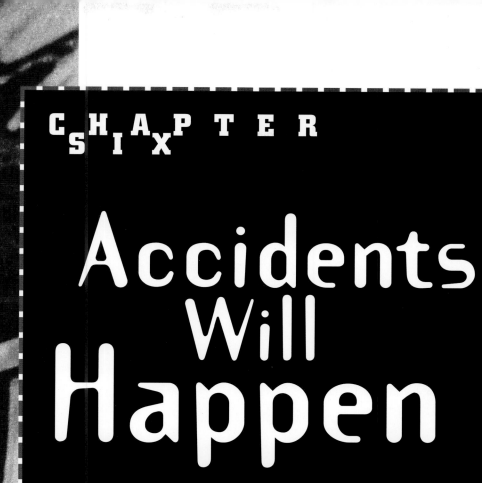

CHAPTER SIX

Accidents Will Happen

HOPE

I

DIE

before

I

get

OLD.

—Pete Townshend, "My Generation"

ecoming famous is often a mixture of talent, hard work, and timing. But talent and hard work may go for naught without timing, and sometimes, timing is everything. And sometimes, the same luck that brings people to fame and fortune turns on

----

them with catastrophic results. Just as stardom can happen suddenly, so can falling out of favor and, as we'll see in this chapter, accidental death.

Roberto Clemente

Pittsburgh Pirates outfielder Roberto Clemente was a phenomenal baseball player. He won four titles for his batting and twelve Gold Gloves for his fielding. He was also voted the National League's

Most Valuable Player in 1966 and, in 1972, became the eleventh man ever to get three thousand hits.

Clemente was also a great humanitarian. He was involved in numerous charities and frequently gave his support to the needy. In 1972, the thirty-eight-year-old baseball star was about to sacrifice his New Year's Day to fly to Nicaragua and distribute supplies to the poverty-stricken survivors of a recent earthquake. On December 31, the DC-7 aircraft carrying Clemente had one engine explode just as it left San Juan Airport. The pilot tried to turn back, but it was too late. Three more explosions ripped through the aircraft, sending it into the Atlantic Ocean. There were no survivors.

On August 6, 1973, Clemente became the first Latin-American player ever to be inducted into baseball's Hall of Fame.

James Dean

James Dean was born on February 8, 1931, in Marion, Indiana. By twenty-one, he was performing on Broadway, and in 1954, his stage work in *The Immoralist* earned him the Theater World Award for Most Promising Newcomer. In 1955, he made his film debut as a troubled teen in *East of Eden*, which brought him to public attention, particularly to the young, who saw the handsome, brooding actor as the embodiment of their own rebellious desires. After earning an Academy Award nomination for his work in *East of Eden*, Dean went on to play yet another troubled youth in *Rebel Without a Cause* (1955). His incredible performance, coupled with the ironic fact that Dean's character meets his death by plunging his automobile over

a cliff, came to symbolize the lost generation of youth of that time—and for generations to follow.

On September 30, 1955, a week after his third and what would be his last movie, *Giant*, finished filming, Dean, who had become quite involved in car racing, set out from Los Angeles to compete in a race in Salinas, California, in his silver Porsche Spyder that he had named "Little Bastard," accompanied by his mechanic and friend (and, some speculate, lover) Rolf Wutherich. At 3:30 P.M., Dean was pulled over for speeding and warned to slow down. At 5:59 P.M., James Dean was doing

DEAN'S PORSCHE SPYDER AFTER THE FATAL ACCIDENT.

— — — — — — — — — — — —

eighty-six miles per hour (138kph) when his Porsche and another car met at an intersection in an explosion of crashing metal.

After the accident, the Porsche looked like a crumpled piece of tinfoil. Wutherich sustained head injuries and a broken leg, the driver of the other vehicle only superficial injuries. Dean, however, was killed instantly.

The tragic death of the twenty-four-year-old idol was a great shock to his fans, who mourned his passing with deep sorrow. They continue to mourn today, making pilgrimages to his grave site, and to worship him through a still-thriving fan club. There is even some have speculation that Dean didn't really die in the accident, but had been so maimed that he was forced into permanent seclusion.

Rebel Without a Cause opened a month after James Dean's death, and *Giant* a year later. The actor received his second Academy Award nomination, for *Giant*, posthumously.

Jon-Erik Hexum

Jon-Erik Hexum's star was just beginning to rise in 1984. The Norwegian hunk had just finished his first motion picture, *Bear*, and, at twenty-six, seemed to have a bright future. On October 12, Hexum was on the set of the television series *Cover Up*, in which he played a fashion photographer–former Green Beret–weapons expert. Just for fun, Hexum picked up a .44 magnum pistol loaded with a blank and held it up to his head a la Russian roulette. Quipping, "Let's see if I got one for me," he pulled the trigger before anyone could stop him. The blank charge at such a close range proved forceful enough to rip through his flesh and send a chunk of skull deep into his brain. The actor was in a coma for six days before doctors declared him brain-dead and family members took him off life support. Emma Samms, who played Cinderella to his Prince Charming on the television show *Hotel*, was at his side. Although friends later suggested he had been uncharacteristically despondent prior to the fatal event, the death of Jon-Erik Hexum was ruled a freak accident.

Buddy Holly, Ritchie Valens, and the Big Bopper

Buddy Holly was already an established rock pioneer in 1959 when his life, along with those of fellow fifties superstars Ritchie Valens and the Big Bopper (J.P. Richardson), was tragically cut short in perhaps the most famous plane crash in rock and roll history.

Twenty-two-year-old Holly, the bespectacled singing-songwriting wonder from Texas, had scored big hits with songs like "Peggy Sue," "That'll Be the Day," and "Oh Boy." Valens, the boy wonder from the Latino streets of Pacoima, California, was just eighteen; his hit "La Bamba" had gone to number three on the pop charts earlier in the year. The first Hispanic to hit the top of the rock charts, Valens was bound for superstardom as well. J.P. Richardson,

DESPITE BUDDY HOLLY'S YOUTH AND EARLY DEMISE, HIS MUSIC INFLUENCED TWO GENERATIONS OF ROCK AND ROLLERS.

DEATH BY FIRE

Jack Cassidy

Jack Cassidy was a Tony Award–winning stage actor, an Emmy Award–winning television actor, and a movie actor whose star was on the rise in the mid-seventies with acclaimed performances in movies like *The Eiger Sanction* (1975) and *W.C. Fields and Me* (1976). He was also the ex-husband of actress Shirley Jones and the father of Shaun and David Cassidy, both teen idols worshiped by girls everywhere. But all that firemen pulled out of the ruins of Jack Cassidy's West Hollywood penthouse after a blazing inferno on December 12, 1976, was an unrecognizable, charred corpse. Since Cassidy had planned a trip to Palm Springs that day and his car was missing, the actor's loved ones initially hoped that the blackened body found on the couch was not his. Unfortunately, his dental records matched the teeth of the corpse. A friend had borrowed the car; Jack had canceled his plans, stayed home, and fallen asleep on the couch. Somehow, a smoldering cigarette fell out of an ashtray onto that very same couch, starting the five-alarm blaze that took the life of the forty-nine-year-old dynamo.

Linda Darnell

Linda Darnell was convinced that burning was a terrible way to go. The young star had just finished a series of movies, including *The Mark of Zorro* (1940) and *Blood and Sand* (1941), with dashing Tyrone Power (who died in 1958 at the age of forty-five after suffering a heart attack while shooting a dueling scene). By 1946, Darnell was a

bona fide movie star. While working on *Anna and the King of Siam* (1946), she had been injured while shooting a scene in which she got burned at the stake. "Never again," she told the press. But in 1947, her character in *Forever Amber* had to be present during the great London fire—Darnell had to be dragged onto the set.

On April 10, 1965, after suffering through three unsuccessful marriages, a waning career, and a drinking problem, Darnell was staying at a friend's house, where she was caught in a fire that was

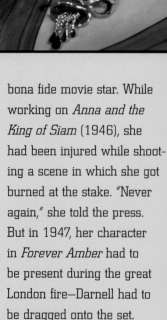

ignited by a burning cigarette left on a couch. Linda was found behind the couch, 80 percent of her upper body covered with second- and third-degree burns. After four hours of surgery, forty-three-year-old Linda Darnell died. Strangely enough, Linda's family had her remains cremated.

OPPOSITE: LINDA DARNELL IN 1940. BELOW: THE FIRE-CHARRED LIVING ROOM IN WHICH DARNELL'S BODY WAS FOUND IN 1965.

better known as the Big Bopper, was riding high from his huge 1958 hit, "Chantilly Lace." The Bopper, who started out as a Texas disc jockey, had developed a stage show based upon his radio persona. He booked Holly and Valens to go with him on a midwestern tour.

The Winter Dance Party Tour was a grueling trip, particularly for Holly, as he was traveling between gigs on drafty buses, then flying to New York

RITCHIE VALENS "WON" A COIN TOSS FOR THE RIGHT TO SIT ON THE DOOMED AIRCRAFT THAT TOOK HIS LIFE.

----

to do recordings in his spare time. On February 3, 1959, disdaining the cold bus ride ahead and hoping to raise the spirits of his band, Holly chartered a

small Beechcraft Bonanza out of Clear Lake, Iowa, to take him to the next show, in Moorhead, Minnesota. Hearing of Holly's plans, the Bopper talked Waylon Jennings (who was accompanying Holly on tour) out of his seat, while Valens won his by flipping a coin with Holly's guitarist, Tommy Allsup. The aircraft took off at 2:00 A.M. in a blinding snowstorm and crashed soon after. The plane hit a fence, taking the lives of all on board. It was this incident that inspired Don McLean's 1972 classic, "American Pie."

Sam Kinison

Sam Kinison was a fire-and-brimstone evangelical preacher for seven years before he found his true calling as a stand-up comic. Kinison's comedy was cynical, profane, and, to many people, offensive. Nonetheless, he had a meteoric rise to fame in 1985 and a huge cult following. In 1987, HBO aired Sam's own show, *Sam Kinison: Breaking the Rules*. Sam's over-the-top stage persona was equaled if not surpassed by his excesses offstage. An avid substance abuser, Sam had a compulsion for just about everything— from red meat to marijuana, from cocaine to womanizing. He was self-indulgent and self-destructive.

By 1992, Kinison was attempting to revamp his act and secure more lucrative mainstream television and film work. The comedian had sworn off drugs, and on April 5, he married his longtime girlfriend, Malika Souiri, a bisexual topless dancer from Las Vegas (who happened to be pregnant at the time).

Five days after his Las Vegas wedding, Kinison booked a comedy gig in Laughlin, Nevada, a thriving riverfront

eight-year-old Sam Kinison died with traces of marijuana, cocaine, codeine, Xanax, and Valium in his system. But ironically, it was this terrible car accident, not his excesses, that finally killed him.

Ernie Kovacs

Ernie Kovacs' bizarre and often sexual humor was well ahead of its time. During his days as a Philadelphia and New York radio talk-show host in the fifties, he lay on active train tracks during one broadcast and hid in a ditch amid rifle-toting hunters during another. Despite (or because of his) quirky behavior, his *Kovacs Unlimited* and *Kovacs on the Corner* shows were successes in the repressed fifties. Although he was notable in several motion picture supporting roles in films such as *Bell, Book, and Candle* (1959) and *Strangers When We Meet* (1960), his greatest and most lasting success was on television, where he starred in *The Ernie Kovacs Show* (1952). He was a unique and offbeat talk-show host, competing with the likes of Steve Allen and Milton Berle.

Kovacs' personal happiness was hampered by his inability to control money. He suffered the financial drain of a nasty divorce, which included a nationwide search for the daughters his ex-wife (née Bette Lee Wilcox) kidnapped, and was also a compulsive gambler with all-around expensive tastes. His second wife, singer Edie Adams, said money "would just go through him like flour through a sieve." He didn't pay taxes for most of his high-profile life. When the Internal Revenue Service finally caught up with him, the debt they called in was more than half a million dollars. Kovacs took

gambling town. Although his manager (and brother) had booked him a plane flight out of Los Angeles, Kinison, who was leery of airplanes, decided to drive the three hundred miles (480km) with his wife instead.

At 7:20 P.M., Sam turned his Trans-Am onto the narrow, curving two-lane highway that was to be the last leg of his journey. A few miles later, his car met with a truck hurtling down the wrong lane. With nowhere to go on the shoulderless road, Kinison tried to swerve off into the desert, but it was too late. In a heaving crash of metal, the Trans-Am was pummeled by the larger vehicle.

COMEDIAN SAM KINISON AND HIS WIFE, MALIKA SOUIRI. KINISON'S FEAR OF FLYING LED TO HIS FATAL DRIVE TO LAUGHLIN, NEVADA.

Kinison's wife suffered a concussion and other minor injuries, but Kinison, who wasn't wearing a seat belt, suffered a fractured skull, a lacerated small bowel, a lacerated heart, and a broken neck. Bleeding internally, he died moments after the crash.

Despite his self-proclaimed desire to move out of the fast lane, thirty-

declined, choosing to leave with Milton Berle and Berle's wife instead.

On his way home, Kovacs attempted to light a cigar with a match, momentarily taking his eyes off the road as he simultaneously sped around a corner. The Corvair careened out of control, hitting a concrete center island, then ricocheting back and slamming into a telephone pole. Kovacs was completely at the mercy of the machine. He was tossed like a rag doll, smacking against the steering column, which flattened his chest, then hitting the dashboard, which crushed his skull and sent portions of bone into his brain. When the car came to rest, Kovacs struggled to free himself, but he was quickly overcome. He died slumped across the front seat, his head hanging out the open passenger door, blood pouring from his nostrils and mouth, his right arm dangling in front of him. Below his right hand, on the pavement, an unlit cigar lay in a growing pool of blood.

Carole Lombard

Carole Lombard had all the chances in the world not to take the plane. The perky blonde star of Hollywood's Golden Age, Lombard appeared in movies such as *Twentieth Century* (1935) and the classic *My Man Godfrey* (1936). In 1942, she volunteered to sell war bonds in Indianapolis in place of her husband, Clark Gable, who had canceled his engagement. On January 15, 1942, the actress and her mother sold over $2 million in war bonds.

The next day, Lombard couldn't decide whether to take a plane or train home to Los Angeles. Her mother,

any job he could, yet still came up short. When he earned $100,000 for one of his later movies (*Sail a Crooked Ship*, 1962), the government took $91,000 right off the top.

By 1962, Kovacs looked tired, haggard, and much older than his forty-two years. On January 13, he spent a long day working on a film, then met Edie for a party at the Beverly Hills home of filmmaker Billy Wilder. Kovacs had several drinks, then decided to leave at 1:20 A.M. He chose to drive Adams' car, a Corvair station wagon, instead of his own Rolls Royce.

ABOVE: ERNIE KOVACS WITH GUEST ON HIS SUCCESSFUL RADIO PROGRAM, *THE ERNIE KOVACS SHOW.* OPPOSITE: ACTRESS CAROLE LOMBARD. AFTER HER DEATH, FRANKLIN D. ROOSEVELT WROTE OF HER, "SHE IS AND ALWAYS WILL BE A STAR, ONE WE SHALL NEVER FORGET, NOR CEASE TO BE GRATEFUL TO."

The couple switched keys. Kovacs kissed Edie goodbye, then offered Yves Montand a ride. The Frenchman politely

OTHER PLANE CRASH VICTIMS

The odds of dying in a plane crash are pretty low, unless you happen to be a musician. The following is a sampling of notables who, unfortunately, beat the odds.

Artist	Patsy Cline	Jim Croce	Rick Nelson	
Group	Soloist	Soloist	Soloist	
Hit Songs	"Crazy," "I'll Fall to Pieces"	"You Don't Mess Around with Jim," "Operator"	"Poor Little Fool," "Fools Rush In," "Travelin' Man," "Garden Party"	
Instrument	Voice	Voice/Guitar	Voice/Guitar	
Type of Plane	Piper Comanche	Piper Comanche	Refurbished Douglas DC-3	
Crash Site	Northeast Hill, Tennessee	Natchitoches, Louisiana	Texarkana, Texas	
Date	March 5, 1963	September 20, 1973	December 29, 1985	
Age	30	30	45	

Otis Redding	Ronnie Van Zant Steve Gaines Cassie Gaines (backup singer) Dean Kirkpatrick (roadie)	Stevie Ray Vaughan
Soloist	Lynryd Skynyrd	Soloist
"(Sittin' by the) Dock of the Bay"	"Free Bird," "Sweet Home Alabama"	"Voodoo Chile (Slight Return)"
Voice	Voice/Guitar	Voice/Guitar
Twin-engine	Convair 240	Bell 206B Jet Ranger helicopter
Lake Monona, Wisconsin	Gillisburg, Mississippi	Alpine Valley Country Club, Illinois
December 10, 1967	October 20, 1977	August 27, 1990
26		35

whose numerologist had forecast the sixteenth as an unlucky day, felt nervous about the flight. Lombard flipped a coin. The plane won out, and Carole, her mother, and her manager boarded along with several other passengers. During a stopover in Albuquerque, New Mexico, Lombard and her companions were asked to await alternate passage to make room on the plane for a group of army aviators. Lombard begged the pilot to let her keep her party aboard until he relented.

The weather turned dismal soon after they left the airport. By the time they reached Nevada, they were in a driving snowstorm. At 7:07 P.M., lost in the blizzard, the plane imploded as it crashed into a rocky mountain near Las Vegas. Two days passed before rescue teams could gain access to the crash site—only then were the mangled corpses recovered. The crash killed twenty passengers, the crew, and thirty-three-year-old Carole Lombard and her mother.

Jayne Mansfield

Jayne Mansfield had an IQ of 163, but her intelligence was overshadowed by her forty-inch (102cm) bustline. Certainly, the star of fifties and sixties comedies such as *The Girl Can't Help It* and *A Guide for the Married Man* did nothing to offset her blonde-bombshell-bimbo image, for she wore the lowest necklines possible, spoke in a babylike whisper, and even appeared twice as a *Playboy* centerfold. By 1967, thirty-five-year-old Mansfield's star was on the decline. She was overweight and bloated from drinking, had suffered two messy divorces, and was becoming

OPPOSITE: Sex symbol Jayne
Mansfield posing for a publicity
shot. BELOW: The wreckage of
Mansfield's car.

Car Fatalities

Car accidents are one of the leading causes of death today, and celebrities are no exception. Perhaps the most unusual automobile-related death is that of **Isadora Duncan**. The modern dance pioneer was driving her sports car in Nice, France, in 1927, when the long scarf that she was wearing became tangled in one of the tires of her car, strangling her almost instantly. She was fifty years old at the time.

Singer **Harry Chapin**, famous for his pop hit "Cat's in the Cradle," was traveling on New York's Long Island Expressway to a benefit concert for one of the numerous charities he supported when his car was struck by a truck in 1980. He was thirty-eight.

Grace Kelly, who starred in Alfred Hitchcock's *Dial M for Murder*, *Rear Window*, and *To Catch a Thief*, and who was married to Prince Rainier III of Monaco, died at fifty-two in 1982 following an automobile accident in which she lost control of her car and careened off a cliff in southern France.

Television news journalist **Jessica Savitch** was killed in 1983 at thirty-six. After spending a relaxing day in New Hope, Pennsylvania, Savitch and her boyfriend, Martin Fishbein, went out for dinner at a restaurant on the other side of the Delaware Canal. When they left, the weather was rainy and extremely foggy. Fishbein took a wrong turn, missed the canal bridge, and drove the car off a cliff into the muddy canal. When rescuers scraped the mud off Savitch's face to identify the body, it was discovered that she had died with her eyes wide open.

involved in the church of Satan. On June 29 at 2:30 A.M., after performing a club engagement in Biloxi, Mississippi, Mansfield, her boyfriend, her three children, and her four pet Chihuahuas set off to New Orleans in a hardtop Buick driven by a college student who worked for the actress. On the rain-slicked highway, just twenty miles (32km) outside New Orleans, the Buick careened headlong into the rear of a truck that had stopped in the middle of the road behind a slow-moving city vehicle, which was spraying the area with insecticide. The impact stripped off the Buick's hardtop and sent the car underneath the trailer truck. The children, who were sleeping in the

---

backseat, suffered only cuts and bruises. But the adults were not so lucky. The college student and the boyfriend were thrown from the vehicle and killed instantly. Mansfield was thrown as well. There is still some controversy as to whether she was beheaded, scalped, or just lost her wig in the fatal crash. In any case, when the car finally came to rest, her blonde hair was still lodged in the dashboard.

Vic Morrow

Vic Morrow made his film debut at the age of twenty-three, as a mean teen in the classic 1955 schoolroom drama, *The Blackboard Jungle*. Among his numerous other credits were *God's Little Acre* (1958), *The Bad News Bears* (1976), and television roles in *The Untouchables*, *The Rifleman*, and *G.E. Theater*. Unfortunately, the gritty character actor is remembered less for his consistently convincing performances than for what happened on the set of his last movie.

After several years of television and stage work, Morrow decided to return to the big screen. In 1982, he took a role in director John Landis' *Twilight Zone—The Movie*. Early in the morning on July 23, Landis and his crew were trying to shoot a complicated scene in which Morrow and two Asian children flee from a helicopter as it fires explosives at them. Landis and his associates chose to use powerful pyrotechnics known as fireballs, to make the scene more "real."

into the ground. Thirty-two-year-old Thurman Munson was killed in the crash. The following night at Yankee Stadium, his uniform number was retired in front of fifty-one thousand fans.

Jackson Pollock

Jackson Pollock was one of the most influential twentieth-century painters and, certainly, the definitive Abstract Expressionist. The works he produced between 1947 and 1952, named by numbers and known as "drip" or "poured" paintings, established his prominence in the art world. *Life* magazine even suggested that Pollock was

At 2:30 A.M., in the middle of filming, shrapnel from the fireballs struck the helicopter, sending it spinning out of control and crashing sideways toward the ground and the actors who were "fleeing" below it. The rotor struck flesh. The two children, six-year-old Renee Shinn Chen and seven-year-old Myca Dinh Lee, were mauled by the blades. Fifty-year-old Vic Morrow was decapitated.

In 1987, John Landis and four staffers were acquitted of involuntary manslaughter charges. Morrow's talent lives on through his youngest daughter, actress Jennifer Jason Leigh.

ABOVE: INVESTIGATORS LOOK OVER THE WRECKAGE OF THE HELICOPTER THAT CRASHED AND KILLED VIC MORROW AND TWO CHILD ACTORS. RIGHT: THE SUMMIT COUNTY CORONER (IN THE STRIPED JACKET) AND OTHERS CONVERSE BY THE RUINS OF THURMAN MUNSON'S SMALL JET PLANE, IN WHICH MUNSON WAS KILLED IN CANTON, OHIO.

Thurman Munson

Catcher Thurman Munson was the captain of three consecutive pennant-winning New York Yankees teams. The first American League catcher ever to win the Rookie of the Year Award, Munson batted over .300 five times in ten years, was an All-Star seven times, and won the Most Valuable Player Award in 1977. His dislike of the press and notorious feuds with prominent adversaries such as Reggie Jackson, George Steinbrenner, and Carlton Fisk created a rowdy public image contrary to Munson's private demeanor. He was a devoted family man—so devoted, in fact, that he bought a small plane in order to spend as much time as possible with his wife and children. Thinking he had fully mastered flying, the catcher bought a jet plane that flew faster than his first. On August 3, 1979, Munson was in Canton, Ohio, and had decided to spend his day off practicing landings in his jet. On one such landing attempt, he lost control and sent the plane careening

"the greatest living painter in the United States." This prestigious recognition came in 1949, after the thirty-seven-year-old artist had spent years living in near-poverty and suffering the derogatory ambivalence of prominent critics. It also came years into his battle with severe depression, which was aggravated by, if not a result of, his chronic alcoholism.

Pollock was notorious for his drinking, of which stories abound. Immediately upon completing his first mural for Peggy Guggenheim, for example, he went to her apartment to await her response to his work. Upon not finding her there, he started drinking. Several hours later, when his benefactor still had not appeared, he stripped naked, crashed a party being given by her roommate, and, in front of several guests, urinated in the fireplace.

Pollack's most productive years were in the late forties, when with the help of his wife, artist Lee Krasner, he abandoned the bottle altogether. But by 1950, artistically burned out and miserably depressed, he began drinking even more ferociously than before. His art suffered, and he moved from dynamism and action to morbidity in his "black" paintings, which are not highly regarded by art critics. He returned to a variation of "drip" painting in his 1954 work *Blue Poles*, now considered one of his greatest works, but then stopped painting altogether.

Pollock's drinking binges further complicated his personal life. On one of his many forays into New York City's late-night tavern scene, he met and took up with a young art student, Ruth Kligman. By July 1956, his devoted wife left for Europe and demanded that he give up his mistress or Krasner would never return.

On Saturday, August 11, after spending the day drinking and crying into his booze, Pollock seemed to cheer up at nightfall. He cooked a steak dinner for Kligman and a friend of hers, Edith Metzger, then suggested he drive them to a New York Philharmonic Orchestra concert in nearby East Hampton. Halfway to the concert, Pollock pulled his Oldsmobile convertible over to the side of the road, claiming he was ill. He then turned the car around and headed home, speeding around sharp curves, prompting Metzger to beg him to let her out of the car. Her plea went ignored, and just a quarter mile (410m) from his home, while rounding another sharp curve, Pollock lost control of the car and sent it hurtling into two small trees. All three passengers were thrown from the convertible. Metzger fell under the car and was crushed to death. Ruth Kligman sustained severe injuries but lived. Jackson Pollock was catapulted, head-first, into one of the trees. His skull collapsed into his brain, and in one instant, the forty-one-year-old artist's self-destructive wish was fulfilled.

Posthumously, Pollock became even more famous, and his work was more increasingly sought after. In 1973, *Blue Poles* sold for $2 million, the most ever paid for the work of an American artist at the time. In the eighties, Andy Warhol lamented with only partial irony, "I wish I had as much money as Jackson Pollock." And in 1984, Krasner died with an estate of $20 million, primarily accumulated through the work of her husband.

Where Are They Now?

Due to the very personal nature of this information, it is impossible for the authors to provide the grave sites of every subject in this book. What follows is a select listing of resting places.

Name	Born	Died	Resting Place
Duane Allman	November 20, 1946	October 29, 1971	Rose Hall Cemetery, Macon, Georgia
Roscoe "Fatty" Arbuckle	March 24, 1887	June 29, 1933	Cremated
Bix Beiderbecke (Leon Bismarck Beiderbecke)	March 10, 1903	August 7, 1931	Oakdale Cemetery, Davenport, Iowa
John Belushi	January 24, 1949	March 5, 1982	Noel's Hill Cemetery, Chilmark, Massachusetts
Lenny Bruce (Leonard Alfred Schneider)	1926	August 3, 1966	Eden Memorial Park, Los Angeles, California
Karen Carpenter	March 2, 1950	February 4, 1983	Forest Lawn Cemetery, Cypress, California
Roberto Clemente	August 18, 1934	December 31, 1972	Lost at sea
Montgomery Clift	October 17, 1920	July 23, 1966	Quaker Cemetery, Brooklyn, New York
Patsy Cline	September 8, 1932	March 5, 1963	Shenandoah Memorial Park, Virginia
Kurt Cobain	February 20, 1967	April 5, 1994	Cremated
Nat "King Cole" (Nathaniel Adams Cole)	March 17, 1919	February 15, 1965	Forest Lawn Cemetery, Glendale, California
Russ Columbo	January 14, 1908	September 2, 1934	Forest Lawn Cemetary, Glendale, California
Bob Crane	July 13, 1928	June 29, 1978	Oakwood Memorial Park, Chatsworth, California

> *And all our yesterdays have lighted fools*
> *The way to dusty death. Out, out, brief candle!*
>
> —William Shakespeare, *Macbeth*

Name	Born	Died	Resting Place
Hart Crane	June 21, 1899	April 27, 1932	Lost at sea
Bobby Darin	May 14, 1936	December 20, 1973	Donated his body to medical research
Linda Darnell (Monetta Elayse Darnell)	October 16, 1921	April 10, 1965	Cremated
James Dean	February 8, 1931	September 30, 1955	Park Cemetery, Fairmount, Indiana
Divine (Harris Glenn Milstead)	October 19, 1945	March 7, 1988	Prospect Hill Cemetery, Towson, Maryland
Dominique Dunne	1960 (?)	November 4, 1982	Westwood Memorial Park, Westwood, California
Amelia Earhart	July 24, 1898	July 3, 1937(?)	Unknown
Brian Epstein	September 19, 1934	August 1967	Jewish Cemetery Long Lane, Aintree, England
Rainer Werner Fassbinder	May 31, 1945	June 10, 1982	Cremated
Judy Garland (Frances Ethel Gumm)	June 10, 1922	June 22, 1969	Ferncliff Cemetery, Hartsdale, New York

Name	Born	Died	Resting Place
Marvin Gaye (**Marvin Pence Gaye, Jr.**)	April 2, 1939	April 1, 1984	Forest Lawn Cemetery, Los Angeles, California
Lou Gehrig (**Henry Louis Gehrig**)	June 19, 1903	June 2, 1941	Kensico Cemetery, Valhalla, New York
Jean Harlow	March 3, 1911	June 7, 1937	Forest Lawn Cemetery, Glendale, California
Jimi Hendrix (**James Marshall**)	November 27, 1942	November 18, 1970	Greenwood Cemetery, Seattle, Washington
Jon-Erik Hexum	November 5, 1957	October 18, 1984	Organ donor
Buddy Holly (**Charles Hardin Holley**)	September 7, 1936	February 3, 1959	Lubbock City Cemetery, Lubbock, Texas
Leslie Howard (**Leslie Stainer**)	April 24, 1890	June 2, 1943	Lost at sea
Sam Kinison	December 8, 1953	April 10, 1992	Tulsa, Oklahoma
Ernie Kovacs	January 23, 1919	January 14, 1962	Forest Lawn Memorial Park, Hollywood Hills, California
Mario Lanza (**Alfred Arnold Cocozza**)	January 31, 1921	October 7, 1959	Holy Cross Cemetery, Los Angeles, California
Brandon Lee	February 1, 1965	March 31, 1993	Lake View Cemetery, Seattle, Washington
Bruce Lee (**Li Yuen Kam**)	November 27, 1940	July 20, 1973	Lake View Cemetery, Seattle, Washington

Name	Born	Died	Resting Place
John Lennon	October 9, 1940	December 8, 1980	Cremated
Carole Lombard (Jane Alice Peters)	October 6, 1908	January 16, 1942	Forest Lawn Cemetery, Glendale, California
Jayne Mansfield (Vera Jayne Palmer)	April 19, 1932	June 29, 1967	Fairview Cemetery, Pen Argyl, Pennsylvania
Bob Marley	April 6, 1945	May 11, 1981	St. Ann's Cemetery, Kingston, Jamaica
Glenn Miller	March 1, 1904	December 15, 1944	Unknown
Sal Mineo	January 10, 1939	February 12, 1976	Cemetery of the Gate of Heaven, Hawthorne, New York
Marilyn Monroe (Norma Jean Mortensen Baker)	June 1, 1926	August 5, 1962	Westwood Memorial Cemetery, Westwood, California
Jim Morrison	December 8, 1943	July 3, 1971	Père LaChaise Cemetery, Paris, France
Vic Morrow	February 14, 1932	July 23, 1982	Mount Olive, Hillside Memorial Park, Los Angeles, California
Rick Nelson	May 8, 1940	December 29, 1985	Forest Lawn Cemetery, Los Angeles, California
Phil Ochs	December 19, 1940	April 9, 1976	Cremated
Heather O'Rourke	December 27, 1975	February 1, 1988	Westwood Memorial Park, Westwood, California
Sylvia Plath	October 27, 1932	February 11, 1963	Heptonstall Churchyard, Yorkshire, England

> *It's not that I'm afraid to die. I just don't want to be there when it happens.*
>
> —Woody Allen

Name	Born	Died	Resting Place
Jackson Pollock	January 28, 1912	August 11, 1956	Green River Cemetery, Springs, New York
Elvis Aron Presley	January 8, 1935	August 16, 1977	Graceland, Memphis, Tennessee
Marie Prevost (Mary Bickford Dunn)	November 8, 1898	January 21, 1937	Cremated
Freddie Prinze (Freddie Preutzel)	June 22, 1954	January 29, 1977	Forest Lawn Memorial Park, Hollywood Hills, California
George Reeves (George Besselo)	April 6, 1914	June 16, 1959	Forest Lawn Cemetery, Glendale, California
Jessica Savitch	February 1, 1947	October 23, 1983	Cremated
Rebecca Schaeffer	November 6, 1967	July 18, 1989	Ahavai Sholom Cemetery, Portland, Oregon
Hillel Slovak	April 13, 1962	July 27, 1988	Mount Sinai Memorial Park, Los Angeles, California
Carl Switzer	August 7, 1927	January 21, 1959	Hollywood Memorial Park, Los Angeles, California
Sharon Tate	January 24, 1943	August 9, 1969	Holy Cross Memorial Park, Culver City, California

Name	Born	Died	Resting Place
William Desmond Taylor (William C. Deane-Tanner)	April 26, 1877	February 1, 1922	Hollywood Memorial Park, Los Angeles, California
Irving Thalberg	May 30, 1899	September 14, 1936	Forest Lawn Cemetery, Glendale, California
Peter Tosh (Winston Hubert Macintosh)	October 19, 1944	September 11, 1987	Kingston, Jamaica
Ritchie Valens (Richard Valenzuela)	May 13, 1941	February 3, 1959	Mission Hill Cemetery, Los Angeles, California
Rudolph Valentino (Rodolfo Alfonzo Raffaelo Pierre Filbert Guglielmi di Valentina d'Antongiolla)	May 6, 1895	August 23, 1926	Hollywood Memorial Park, Los Angeles, California
Stevie Ray Vaughan	October 3, 1954	August 27, 1990	Laurel Land Cemetery, Dallas, Texas
Thomas "Fats" Waller	May 21, 1904	December 15, 1943	Cremated
Hank Williams (Hiram King Williams)	September 17, 1923	January 1, 1953	Oakwood Annex, Virginia
Natalie Wood (Natasha Nikolaeuna)	July 20, 1938	November 29, 1981	Westwood Memorial Cemetary, Westwood, California
Virginia Woolf	January 25, 1882	March 28, 1941	Cremated

Bibliography

Anger, Kenneth. *Hollywood Babylon.* New York: Bell Publishing Company, 1975.

Austin, John. *Hollywood's Unsolved Mysteries.* New York: Shapolsky Publishers, Inc., 1990.

Barbour, John A., and Maria Pruetzel. *The Freddie Prinze Story.* Kalamazoo, Mich.: Master's Press, Inc., 1978.

Bresker, Fenton. *Who Killed John Lennon?* New York: St. Martin's Press, 1989.

Briand, Paul L., Jr. *Daughter of the Sky: The Story of Amelia Earhart.* New York: Van Rees Press, 1960.

Brown, Peter Harry, and Patte B. Barham. *Marilyn: The Last Take.* New York: E.P. Dutton, 1992.

Clifford, Mike. *The Harmony Illustrated Encyclopedia of Rock.* New York: Harmony Books, 1988.

Cole, Bill. *John Coltrane.* New York: Schirmer Books, 1976.

Culbertson, Judi, and Tom Randall. *Permanent Californians: An Illustrated Guide to the Cemeteries of California.* Chelsea, Vt.: Chelsea Green Publishing Co., 1989.

DiOrio, Al. *Borrowed Time: The 37 Years of Bobby Darin.* Philadelphia: Running Press, 1981.

Escott, Colin, with George Merritt and William MacEwen. *Hank Williams: The Biography.* Boston: Little, Brown, 1994.

Feather, Leonard. *The Encyclopedia of Jazz.* New York: Bonanza Books, 1955.

Goerner, Fred. *The Search for Amelia Earhart.* New York: Doubleday, 1966.

Harris, Warren G. *Natalie & R.J.: Hollywood's Star-Crossed Lovers.* Garden City, N.Y.: Doubleday, 1988.

Heatley, Michael, ed. *The Ultimate Encyclopedia of Rock.* New York: HarperCollins, 1993.

Katz, Robert. *Love Is Colder than Death: The Life and Times of Rainer Werner Fassbinder.* New York: Random House, 1987.

Kinison, Bill, with Steve Delsohn. *Brother Sam: The Short, Spectacular Life of Sam Kinison.* New York: William Morrow & Co., 1994.

Lamparski, Richard. *Lamparski's Hidden Hollywood.* New York: Simon & Schuster, 1981.

Miller, Jim, ed. *The Rolling Stone Illustrated History of Rock and Roll.* New York: Random House, 1976.

Morris, Jeannie. *Brian Piccolo: A Short Season.* New York: Rand McNally, 1971.

Munn, Michael. *The Hollywood Murder Casebook.* New York: St. Martin's Press, 1987.

Musick, Phil. *Who Was Roberto? A Biography of Roberto Clemente.* Garden City, N.Y.: Doubleday, 1974.

O'Meally, Robert G. *Lady Day: The Many Faces of Billie Holiday.* New York: Arcade Publishing, 1991.

Pareles, Jon, and Patricia Romanowski, eds. *The Rolling Stone Encyclopedia of Rock and Roll.* New York: Summit Books, 1993.

Parish, James Robert. *The Hollywood Celebrity Death Book.* Las Vegas, Nev.: Pioneer Books, 1993.

Peary, Dan, ed. *Cult Baseball Players, The Greats, The Flakes, The Weird and The Wonderful.* New York: Simon & Schuster, 1990.

Reisner, Robert George. *Bird: The Legend of Charlie Parker.* New York: The Citadel Press, 1962.

Robinson, Ray. *Iron Horse: Lou Gehrig in His Time.* New York: W.W. Norton, 1990.

Rolling Stone magazine editors. *Cobain.* Boston: Little, Brown, 1994.

Schessler, Ken. *Ken Schessler's This Is Hollywood: An Unusual Movieland Guide.* La Verne, Calif: Ken Schessler Publishing, 1978.

Scott, Michael. *The Great Caruso.* New York: Knopf, 1988.

Solomon, Deborah. *Jackson Pollock: A Biography.* New York: Simon & Schuster, 1987.

Stein, Jean, ed., with George Plimpton. *Edie: An American Biography.* New York: Knopf, 1982.

Summers, Anthony. *Goddess: The Secret Lives of Marilyn Monroe.* New York: Macmillan, 1985.

Thomson, Elizabeth, and David Gutman, eds. *The Lennon Companion: Twenty-Five Years of Comment.* New York: Schirmer Books, Inc., 1987.

Wagner-Martin, Linda. *Sylvia Plath: A Biography.* New York: Simon & Schuster, 1987.

Wolf, Marvin J., and Katherine Mader. *Fallen Angels: Chronicles of L.A. Crime and Mystery.* New York: Facts on File, 1986.

Wood, Lana. *Natalie.* Toronto: General Publishing Co., 1984.

Photography Credits

© AP/Wide World Photos: pp.13 both, 24, 26 bottom, 33 bottom, 35, 40 bottom, 45, 72 bottom, 100, 103, 105, 106, 116 top, 117
© Bettman Archive: pp. 14, 20, 22 top, 25, 38, 39, 52, 64, 67, 79 top, 87, 101
Globe Photos: pp. 114, 115; © Stephen Allen: p. 84 top; © Claxton: p. 73; © Henry Diitz: p. 54; © Ralph Dominguez: p. 36 right; © Tony Esparza: p. 80; © Patrick LaBanca: p. 76; © G. Merrin: p. 57 bottom; © Doris Nieh: p. 17; © NBC: pp. 48, 60, 86, 97, 108; © Adam Scull/Rangefinders: p. 68–69; © SMP: pp. 29 top, 78; © Sterling/MacFadden: p. 111; Courtesy of Charles Stewart, photograph by Herman Leonard: p. 50; © Dan Tompkins: p. 23
© Dave Hogan/REX Features, London: p. 91
© The Kobal Collection: pp. 2, 6, 12, 19, 27, 37, 40 top, 53, 56, 65 top, 104, 109, 112
© London Features International: p. 66; © Kevin Mazur: p. 88; © Kevin Cummins: p. 93 top
© Neal Peters Collection: p. 70
© Photofest: pp. 8–9, 30–31, 32, 36 left, 61, 94
© Ramey Photo Agency: p. 84 bottom
Retna, Ltd.: © A.J. Barratt: p. 92; © David Corio: p. 62–63; © Doc Pele/Stills: pp. 15, 68 left, 75, 77, 98; © Tom Hanley/Camera Press: p. 34; © Walter McBride: p. 57 top; © Terry O'Neill/Camera Press: p. 41; © Michael Putland: pp. 69 right, 93 left
Star File: © Ron Delaney: p. 55; © Jerry Wolfe: p. 33 top; ©Vince Zuffante: p. 107

© UPI/Bettman: pp. 10–11, 16, 21 both, 22 bottom, 26 top, 28–29, 42, 43, 44, 46, 49, 51, 58–59, 65 bottom, 72 top, 79 bottom, 81, 95, 102, 113

Index